LIVING ON AIR

A RADIOGIRL'S QUEST FOR FAIRNESS AND HAPPILY EVER AFTER

Allyson Martinek

all my best,
allyson

Edited by Cheri L. R. Taylor

Layout by T. Andrew Caddick

Cover Art by Fred Tovich

ISBN-13: 978-1522764779

ISBN-10: 1522764771

ACKNOWLEDGMENTS

Kevin Metheny, when I think of all we could have done together if only we'd met earlier. I can't thank you enough for your support and love, and for all you tried to do for me and for my show. I'll never forget your words "When I get settled I'll send for help." The world lost a beautiful soul much too soon, and I lost an ally and a friend.

• • • • •

We're a small family but we get the job done. And from the beginning it's always been just the three of us, fiercely tight and devoted to each other. Because I have my mom and my sister I am never alone and never without. When one is in need the other two drop everything, and that's just how we roll. Three different last names, one giant heart, I love you Mom and Jill.

• • • • •

"Why don't you two get married?"

Oh, if only we had a dime for every time we've heard it. Our standard answer is "We'll marry when there is world peace," but we live by "if it ain't broke why fix it?" And in 23 years it "aint" broke yet. You sat in the car for hours while I did my first air shift, you drove me in every snow storm that terrified me, you do all the heavy lifting AND steam cleaning, and you happily accept that there will only be dinner if you make it. And you didn't flinch at these two words: bed pan. That's a soul mate. You're my best friend and I'm proud to call you my "baby daddy." To Warren, all of my love.

• • • • •

It is my honor and my privilege to every day be a part of Detroit's rich tapestry. I love this city, its determination, its spirit. Detroit's story helped shape and define my own story, and for that I feel fortunate. It's like being a member of a secret cool club, and the pride that comes from being chosen.

It's a Detroit thing!

I don't know if it's possible to say thank you too much. Does it get annoying at a certain point? It's possible I may have reached that point. On social media, in videos, through personal messages, throughout these pages, I've expressed my unwavering gratitude to my listeners, my audience, my now extended family. I have such gratitude for allowing me to share my life with you every day, and for the love you showered me with when I needed it most. With smiley faces, and exclamation points and pizza slice emojis, here's one more for good measure: THANK YOU!

Allyson

INTRODUCTION

I purchased a piece of artwork a couple of years ago. It's a bright white canvas/print with different phrases covering the entire square. "Choose Happiness" is written in bold black letters dead center. It's an inspirational piece of art, meant to uplift. "Choose Happiness" reminds us that it really is a choice, that we get to make that decision for ourselves.

Surrounding "Choose Happiness" and written in gray, the rest of the print reads: "You are the real thing, a genuine original, perfect in all your flaws, so find your voice and change the world. Make a real difference. Be a hero, an inspiration, a mentor. Believe in your gifts and use them wisely. Never stop asking questions. Embrace the journey. Be passionate about things that matter most to you. Follow your heart. Remember that true beauty lies in your capacity to love. Strive to be the best version of yourself. Demonstrate character. Be brave and fearless. Find inspiration everywhere. Don't let anyone hold you back. Believe you can do anything and you will. Your life is now. Become the person you were destined to be. Be kind not only to yourself but to others. Be bold. Take risks. Embrace your individuality it is the only thing that sets you apart in the world. Stand for something bigger than yourself. Listen to your intuition. Look at life through the lens of your heart, it is the only compass you need. You are the author of your own life story, make it a good one."

I know, a wordy piece of art, right? It hung on my bedroom wall for years, now I found myself more intently focused on it like never before.

Some pretty wonderful directives were printed across that canvas—soul nurturing stuff. Then one day it just jumped out at me, the very last phrase on that print, "Be the author of your own life story, make it a good one."

YES! DO THAT!

I'm my own author. I wasn't going to let someone else decide

MY story. There was no way in hell THEY would have the last word.

"Don't lose sight now Allyson. You don't take that kind of crap, snap out of it! Remember who you are and what you stand for. You do Kim Kardashian impressions and you stand up for the little guy, even when the little guy is you."

My inner voice can be bossy sometimes.

"Be the author of your own story, make it a good one."

Oh, and it's a good one alright, it's even got Oprah in it. And it's only getting started. Maybe by sharing my story, I could remind others to be their own authors, too. Prove that you CAN make your wildest dreams come true, that what you put out into the world will come back to you, and that with hard work and determination there are no limits to what you can achieve.

After all, I did it.

When it's the thing you want the most, anyone can do it! And that's just the first half of my story. I have so many chapters left, blank pieces of paper to fill with so many purposeful moments. And let's be honest, pointless silly moments too, (probably pretty heavy on the latter).

Not every part of the story is going to be something we can control. There will always be the jerks in suits and the sociopaths on heels. We can't control when we'll encounter someone in life in the right position to yank the rug right out from under us, as unfortunately, bad people are real. But all of the rest? How we pick back up, become better than we ever were before, and never stop achieving our wildest dreams? Yeah, that's all us!

I don't know exactly how the next chapter of my story begins, but I know one thing, it's going to be good. I'm the author of my own story, and I'm going to make it a good one. I hope sharing mine causes smiles, some giggles and if you're in need of inspiration or encouragement, I hope you'll find that here too.

Don't be afraid to ask the universe for what you want, don't be afraid to do things your own way, and never let anyone else determine your fate.

Chapter One

SHOCK AND AWE...WITHOUT THE AWE.

You hear people talk about that feeling of being in shock.

Everything moves in slow motion. You see mouths moving, but you don't hear words. An inexplicable pit in your stomach leaves you feeling as if you'd been punched.

Shock.

Total shock!

It was a random Monday morning, and I was fresh back from a week long summer vacation. I had just finished my morning show—my very successful morning show, the one I'd been doing for ten years in the city of Detroit, at the radio station where I had worked at for twenty years. The radio station that I had more than helped to build in my lengthy tenure.

I had been off the week before, and Best Of shows had played in my absence. So on this Monday morning, I was eager to get back to it, and to interact with my audience. That's the part of my job I love the most—connecting with the listeners. I share my life stories with them, and hear about theirs in return.

Even on vacation I could be found on various social media sites, keeping everyone updated on every mundane (yet riveting) moment of my life. But, it was good to be back talking! I was broadcasting interesting tidbits from my weeklong summer vacation, and doing what I do—talking and being silly on the radio. It's where I'm the most comfortable.

And this Monday morning, I was refreshed, recharged, and happy to be back!

My show ended the same time it always did, just before 10 a.m. When the next host assumed control, I would record some promos and plan the next day's show. Then I'd be done for the day, until we met again tomorrow. I was sitting in my chair, talking with some co-workers, when a manager came into the studio. He tapped me on my shoulder and said, "You got a minute?"

"Absolutely," I said, beaming.

I had been acquainted with this manager for about a years time, and despite numerous red flags that would soon become apparent to me, we had a good relationship. At that moment I thought what he wanted was to pick up where we had left off in a previous discussion that took place right before my week long vacation, so I was eager to comply.

Over the course of the past year we had many discussions regarding a serious problem that existed at the station, that not just me, but almost everyone was aware of. Anything that I could do to help get us closure on this issue was something I was more than happy to do. So, up out of my chair I went, and out of the studio I followed.

When we exited the room, I expected him to grab another empty studio, somewhere we could talk privately. We had done this before, so I assumed that once again, we would dart into the closest room.

We were a few steps out of the studio, yet this was not happening. There were rooms directly across the hall, and all around us, yet he kept walking down the hallway, farther away from rooms where we could talk. A flash of panic came over me, but soon passed, when I then assumed we must be heading to his office. These thoughts and feelings were happening in milliseconds, as it didn't take long to get to the end of the hallway, and to the bottom of the ramp, where he suddenly took a right turn.

I was several steps behind him and my heart dropped when I saw the right turn. His office was in the opposite direction. Everything was in the opposite direction.

There was only one thing off to the right at the end of the hall —the Human Resources office.

My brain started to scramble as I realized that this was where we were going. I kept grasping at any straws that might be left. Could it be something else? Maybe I'm overreacting? As I mentioned, we had an existing problem at the station. It was a serious one, as far as almost all of us were concerned, and it was the subject matter of his and my last conversation, so maybe we were going to the HR office to discuss that? Maybe my statements were needed to start the ball rolling on solving that problem?

Yep, my heart was hanging in there, trying to come up with any reason this could be anything other than what it was. Surely, this organization that had been my home for more than 20 years had more respect for me than to simply fire me with no notice, and no prior discussion. Surely, my contributions here were worth far more than that sort of off-handed dumping? My optimistic heart was soon to crash, and hard.

I was being fired.

Right now.

Just like that.

I had never been fired before. I'd never been fired in my radio career, or from ANY job I'd held growing up prior to my career. I had however, heard tales about how firing in radio "went down."

It happened in front of the HR person, and then you would be walked out of the building, and other wonderful, "non-humiliating" actions that pertain to the event.

But, I couldn't be fired! I hadn't done anything wrong.

I wasn't just one of the most well known personalities at this station, but in the city of Detroit, as well. Heck, across the country. And damn it, even in Canada!

This was when the shock set in. Who was this man to come in and destroy that? Especially when I hadn't done anything wrong.

Just a year and half earlier a different manager was in charge. He was a legend in the industry. A very well-known actor even played him in the movie about a famous shock jock. And this man was a good friend to me, and loved my show. He knew about the issues we were having, and was going to help. But, as things often happen, he was transferred before he could help, and my heart broke. We were SO close to ending the bullshit here. One of the last things he said to me was "I'll send for help when I get situated."

He died just a couple of months later. It was a devastating loss; he was a wonderful man who died much too soon, and I lost a friend and an ally. Enter this guy, the firing guy, who decided he had the right to end my 20 year career. Everything that I had built was snatched away.

As we sat in the HR office, he continued to explain his reasons. A bunch of nonsense babble came out of the manager's mouth about rebranding and it affecting my position immediately. I knew better. This wasn't about rebranding, this was personal! Everything on my morning show was staying exactly the same, with one exception; the person who built the show was being fired.

I looked at this man and said, "Do you have any idea what you're doing?"

I suspected, at that moment, that he didn't. He was about to break up a show that had achieved national attention! It was a show that for 10 years, had been one of the most popular, and highest rated shows in Detroit, and had an extremely loyal following.

I was the reason for that.

Oh, and the cherry on the sundae here is that I had just three weeks prior, celebrated my 20 year anniversary with the station. This is a feat that is not often duplicated. For one person to sustain a career in radio at the same station for two decades is almost unheard of.

And it was something I couldn't have been more proud of!

I was literally still receiving emails of congratulations. Just three weeks earlier, we were celebrating that milestone on my show, and now this jerk in a suit and a sociopath in heels, were putting an end to all I had built.

All I had built for myself. All I had built for them.

Shock.

I was in shock that in the blink of an eye, something that I had worked so hard for, something that mattered not just to me, but to so many people, was about to be gone. It was shock that all of this could happen because one damaging individual in the right position, not only wanted this, but had set her sights on it years earlier.

I couldn't really hear words anymore. This ball was in motion and there was no stopping it.

I remember looking at the friendly face in the HR chair, and even she looked shocked. I needed to read some paperwork and sign it. I think that's what the jerk in the suit kept saying. I just wanted to get out of there. If this was happening, then I wanted to put this toxic place and the two toxic individuals who'd created this horrible moment behind me for good.

I grabbed the paperwork and we headed back to the studio, back to MY studio, so I could get my purse and turn my entry card over to him —the card that opened the doors to this beautiful building for me for the last 20 years.

"We'll box your stuff up," he said.

I interrupted him with, "You can cram all my stuff."

I'm pretty sure I said that. At least, I hope I did, because boy did I want him to cram it! Because of the shock and my inability to hear much of anything anymore, I can't be sure, but I think he said something along the lines of calling me to check on me in a few days.

Really?! You just destroyed my 20 year career for personal reasons. The last thing you should even think about doing is calling my phone.

Ever.

So, to recap:

One—you can cram all of my stuff, including my Cat Mom coffee mug, and two—forget you ever knew my phone number, because you and I, Sir, have had our last interaction for our duration on this planet.

I grabbed my purse and headed back down the same hallway, walking with definite purpose. He was not going to escort me out of any building. He could walk behind me.

And I exited the frosty glass doors for the very last time. I took the elevator down to the gorgeous marbled lobby for the very last time, and drove my car out of the parking garage for the very last time.

I gave my daily wink and wave to the garage attendant, like I did every day, knowing it would be the last time we smiled "Have a good day," to each other.

And then I bawled my eyes out.

I was driving away from my radio home and for the first time, in my adult life, I didn't have a job. I didn't have benefits. I didn't have anywhere to go tomorrow or for all the days after.

I was lost.

My commute from the radio station to my apartment was around thirty minutes, and I'll be damned if I remember being on the expressway for even a minute. I had pulled out of the garage at the station and the next minute, I was sitting in front of my apartment building. The shock was still so strong, I didn't remember driving home. I try to be a safe and attentive driver! I'm just glad it all worked out.

I sat in front of my building knowing I had to go in and break this news to the people closest to me. I had to do this knowing that they weren't just going to be sad for me, but would also now carry their own worries for the future, and that was a hard pill to swallow.

When I had stalled enough, it was time to get out of the car. In the building, and up the stairs I went. I put my key in the door and opened it.

There was my boyfriend, my life partner of 24 years, who'd been present from the inception of this illustrious career, sitting on the sofa. He was more than familiar with the "bad guys" at work.

We looked at each other and he knew. He knew the way you know people and things after spending that much time together. He knew. And before I had the front door shut, he made his way to me and we just started hugging the grief away.

I wasn't crying any more. I had to be strong. I had become the primary breadwinner in our relationship, and I didn't want him to worry. I wasn't going to worry.

The reality of my severance was setting in though. There were only going to be a few more checks coming my way. OUCH! That should be cause for worry, but I knew we would be okay. I had built an amazing career for myself, through hard work and a little push from destiny. And those two at the station would not have the final say on my future. I was the author of my story and the best was truly going to be…yet to come.

Those people, that place, they weren't getting one more ounce of energy from me. So, while it was true that I only had a handful of checks that would still be coming my way, I knew we would be okay.

I had built an amazing career for myself, through hard work and a little push from destiny. And those two clueless fools would not have the final say on my future.

I am the author of my story, and the best was, and is, yet to come.

Chapter Two

BE CAREFUL WHAT YOU WISH FOR

I'm a huge believer in karma, in destiny, the universe, the art of attraction, in God. And I've always felt guided, not just through my career, but through life in general. It's hard to explain without sounding crazy, but I've just always felt "not alone," and that things in my life were really meant to be. Maybe it's because I grew up with hippy parents and Buddhas and crystals were peppered throughout my childhood home.

I believe you have to use your voice and your platform to help others. I believe in "I am my brothers keeper" and "be the change you want to see in the world." I know that sounds like positive mumbo jumbo, but I've tried to apply this throughout my career. I had a voice on the radio, and I wanted to make sure that I used it to benefit others.

Don't get me wrong, I absolutely love the other perks of my job! I got to talk to Oprah on the phone for goodness sake! I go on press junkets. I travel. I've become friends with celebrities, and even had a TV show. Those are amazing experiences! But, the part of my job that brings me the most joy is being able to make a difference in someone's life! And I put that out there every day!

The things that happened next in my story are proof that destiny is real, and that when you put goodness out into the world, it comes back to you.

It started with the Sunday night before going back to work. My vacation was coming to an end and the following morning I was back on the air. About a year and a half earlier, I had made a vision board. As I mentioned, things had been difficult at work for some time. It just takes one toxic person and the next thing you know the coolest job in the world isn't as fun anymore. Things desperately needed to change. Intentional roadblocks were impacting my career and causing my show to suffer.

Negative people can have that affect.

So, I made the vision board and I put sayings on it like:

The best is yet to come.

Your star is on the rise.

Believe in miracles.

I've come too far not to win.

Big things are coming for your career.

Schmaltzy? Maybe, but I'm into that.

The night before I returned to work, I really meditated on it. I mean, I had been meditating throughout, but that Sunday night, I REALLY focused on it. I had just recharged on vacation, and was about to go back into this, for lack of a better word, blaaaaah-ness that had been plaguing me, and the show for some time, so I took the vision board out for a spin. And I told God, and my Grandma, the universe, and any other guardian angels I may have, that I desperately needed these "sayings" to manifest in my life. Too much time had been wasted. I was ready for the next step. I was ready for the best that was yet to come. When I was done appealing to the universe, I climbed into bed and called it a night!

The next morning I was fired after my show!

Did I wish for this? Was I getting exactly what I asked for? Had I gone as far as I could at this place? All signs pointed to yes. And although I would have never left my job on my own, there was a freeing feeling that came along with this sudden change. Although I knew I had very few paychecks left to rely on, I was eerily calm, as if the universe was saying, "I'm not even going to let you worry about this girl! You got this!" (That's how I imagine the universe talks.)

I would have stayed forever, allowing whatever poor treatment and disrespect I was receiving to continue. And it's not because I don't think I deserve better. I'm a strong woman who's taken charge my entire life, but sometimes even the strongest of us have clouded judgement. We put other people before ourselves, thinking that it's the right thing to do.

Anytime I had an opportunity to branch out, to take a better opportunity with better pay, I'd worry about the people I was leaving behind. It was important to me not to be disloyal. So, you can be strong and misguided at the same time. That's when God or the universe or whatever force of good you believe in, steps in. Destiny is real, and things do happen for a reason. So, I may have gotten just what I asked for.

The next thing that happened proved that putting good into the world will cause it to come right back to you. And it was the most amazing thing I've ever experienced in my life.

I knew on that Monday morning that in 24 hours, everyone would know I was gone. My audience would know, the city of Detroit, the state of Michigan, across the country, and Canada, too! Everyone would know that I was no longer on the air.

After 10 years of waking up the city, and 20 years of keeping good company, *POOF*—just like that, I was gone!

I knew that I had built a really great relationship with my audience. I cared about them and they cared about me, too! And I knew there would be some "backlash" to this ridiculous decision to remove me, but I had no idea of what would happen within 24 hours of my removal becoming news! My family joked that I had " broken the internet."

The messages started coming through social media in a way I

never could have imagined. I knew people would reach out asking the normal questions, "What happened?" "Why aren't you there anymore?", "Where can I hear you now?" Some would send messages of being sad, that they would miss me. I expected some of that. Some.

But thousands of messages came in from people I didn't even know listened to my show! Messages came from every single state in the country.

They were messages that brought tears to my eyes!

People were worried about me, about my family, about my cats! My listeners offered me money, meals, friendship and an actual shoulder to cry on. They offered their personal time, their homes, medical and dental care, rides to places—just things you don't expect to hear from anyone, let alone total strangers!

But, the thing is, they weren't strangers! They'd been listening to me for a very long time, and I was their friend, even though we'd never met.

And I knew then that the one thing I always really cared about in my radio career—making genuine connections, had come through on the other end of the radio. I could have been just another person on the radio who wasn't there anymore, but I wasn't. I was their FRIEND, who was being replaced, and they were letting me and everyone else know how they felt!

I couldn't have felt more fortunate and blessed!

Other people can't control our destiny. Greater forces help us along. And our hard work and our good work can't be silenced. At a time when someone tried to silence my voice, it caused so many others to speak out!

No matter what your platform is in life, if you're on the radio, or work in the library, do peoples taxes, bake cakes, clean teeth, CEO something, you can make a difference in someone else's life! And when you do, you might find it coming back to you when you need it the most.

I'll never forget the heartfelt messages I received in my time of need and I can't say thank you enough to all of my dear friends that I've never met. Thank you for being there for me. It means more than I can ever say.

When I was at my lowest, people I thought were my friends were not. But look at ALL of these amazing friends I found! I was going to be okay. How could I not be okay? I had thousands of messages in front of me telling me the best was yet to come.

Chapter Three

BEER KEGS, BOYFRIENDS AND BROADCASTING, OH MY

The theme throughout my career has been, "This is your destiny," because I had completely different plans for my future. Sometimes the plan for you is not the plan you have for yourself. I started college intending to be a high school teacher, or possibly a college professor. I figured that since I had crushed high school as a student, teaching it would be the perfect career choice. Oh and by "crushed it" that doesn't mean I got good grades, it means I had really fantastic, feathered hair.

I come from a radio family but I never thought of radio as anything other than something you listened to. Despite my mother's initial being included in radio call letters, WJML, (she's the L) a career in radio never crossed my mind. Not once. It all started as—what's the saying? A happy accident.

It turns out that quarter beer night can actually negatively affect your grades. I really didn't like to miss quarter beer night, so after my first year of college my GPA really hit the skids. My plan to transfer from one university to another was put on hold in light of my new grade "situation". The university I was applying to was going to require me to bring up the average, a request easy to comply with. I'd have to go to the local community college for a semester, make grades a priority this time, and I'd officially be a student at said university.

So I had a plan, moved into a house on campus, and got ready to straighten up and fly right, as they say. (If they still say that.) Like lots of people my age, I was really into music. I spent a lot of time listening to music, shopping at record stores, and going to concerts. Alternative music was my thing. My favorite band was the Cure. Oh if only "right now" Allyson knew that "future" Allyson was going to meet the band and have the lead singer flirt with her she'd FREAK OUT!

I loved The Smiths, INXS, Depeche Mode—basically any kind of music that fit under the "alternative" umbrella. At that time there was no radio station in the area that catered to those musical tastes, so people into that scene relied on their own CD's and—wait for it—cassette tapes.

At the same time that I was making my life/school changes, an alternative radio station popped up on the dial! Out of the blue! It was brand new and there was nothing like it in Detroit. There were obviously college alternative stations around the state, but this was a full blown commercial radio station that played every single band I liked—and then some! I fell in love. It was like discovering the radio for the first time despite having listened to it all my life. Now radio had my attention and the seed to be involved with it had been planted. I never considered broadcasting as a career, but these new feelings would change my college plans—just slightly.

I discovered that there was a broadcast arts school in the city. Seriously? A school that taught radio? This was happening. It was a nine month program that prepared you for a career in radio or television and completing it would satisfy my grade point average issues.

How amazing was this?

I wouldn't have to go to community college, I could learn about radio and earn credits that transferred directly to the university. I could accomplish my goals while learning more about this "possible" new career choice. The credits transferring sealed the deal.

Although my head was in the clouds over a possible radio career, I was still realistically following my plan to be a teacher. So I contacted the school, took an entrance exam, filled out the paperwork, and destiny's plan was set in motion. I was now a student at the broadcast arts school! I commuted daily from my house on campus into the city while listening to, and being fueled by, my favorite new alternative radio station. It was a busy time for me. I was going to school Monday through Friday all day and waiting tables at a local steak house in the evening. Quarter beer night was still going on a few streets from my house, but this time I was more focused than I'd ever been. So I only went occasionally. (It's a QUARTER, how do you pass that up?)

Right around this time I met a boy, a boy named Warren. The house I lived in had become, and I don't like to brag, but kind of legendary for our "after" parties. The bar closed and the party moved to our house. People just knew that. It was at one of those parties where our eyes met over a beer keg, which is where all good love stories start. A relationship began at that very moment. He spent the night that night, and we were never apart again.

I'd like my mom to know that he slept on the couch, of course.

It's funny the way things work, because at this time in my life I was NOT looking for a relationship—at all! I had two previous relationships that I thought would absolutely lead to marriage, but instead both ended in heartbreak. Mine. So I had zero plans to fall in love with anyone again. I was protecting what was left of my heart and, I won't lie, I was enjoying the single life. I was also really busy, and extremely focused. I was immersed in school, and I was working almost every night waiting tables. So my plan on the night we met was to be casual. Warren's plan was different. And despite my ambitious goals for the future, he wanted to be a part of my life. Whether I was ready for it or not I was now officially in a relationship.

Over the next nine months I soaked in everything I could about the radio industry. I was flourishing in the program and it was becoming clear I had a natural ability to do this as a career. Yes, I was still thinking "teacher", but I was flirting more and more with radio. And I made my wish list known to the placement department of the broadcast school. I would visit the ladies working there regularly and share with them my love for this new alternative radio station. I was obsessed, and wanted to work there. As a matter of fact, I really only wanted a radio career if I could work at THAT station. This was a very narrow vision, its true, but my laser focus paid off.

In May of that year, school had come to an end, and I graduated with high marks. I even threw one heck of a graduation party for my class at my house on campus. It was the party house after all, so it only seemed fitting. And in true legendary party house fashion, the party was even shut down by the police. I showed my classmates how to graduate with a bang.

I really thrived in the broadcast program and was ready for the next chapter of life. While I was filled with radio dreams, I still planned to send my transcripts to the university and enroll for fall semester. But before any of that could happen my phone rang. It was literally just days after graduation. I don't think I'd even finished cleaning up from the party. It was one of the wonderful ladies from the placement department. It turns out that my constant visits and droning on about that "alternative radio station" weren't in vain. She was on the other end of the phone with a job lead, a lead that caused her to immediately think of me. As a matter of fact, she was giving me a head start on the lead before she made it public to all. She just had a feeling about me for this job, she said.

I wasn't going to waste any time, I went into pounce mode! The information she was giving me was extremely familiar. I knew the name she was giving me.

I knew that name!

I was over the moon. This was going to happen.

Knock-knock.

Who's there?

Destiny, again.

Chapter Four

WE'RE MOVING ON UP... TO THE WEST SIDE

I couldn't believe who I was about to meet! I followed up on the job lead I'd been given the second I hung up the phone. I knew who the employer was, and I was determined to get this job. In the blink of an eye, the call was placed, the interview was scheduled, and I was out the door. I had a 90 minute car ride to shake off the nervous energy and get it together. I was about to meet the man who founded the alternative radio station in Detroit that I loved so much; the radio station that completely inspired me to rearrange my school plans. HIM! Not only had he created the Detroit station, he also hosted the morning show, and now he was about to start a second station in the states capitol.

There's a real advantage to having a genuine enthusiasm for the job you're applying for, and I was armed with information and ready to WOW. It was then I met Greg. For me it was equal to meeting a celebrity, but thankfully I was able to keep my fawning to a minimum. The interview began, and I proceeded to tell him every single thing about his Detroit radio station. I knew the day it debuted on the air. I knew every feature they did, every personality who worked there, and every minor detail about this radio station. And I didn't know these things because I'd researched it. Greg knew that I had been eating, sleeping, and breathing that radio station, and I was hired on the spot. There was no, "We'll let you know in a few days." That job was mine by the time I walked out the door.

Greg and I hit it off right away, and he became my first mentor. He would play a big part in the journey I was about to begin. I went home and shared the news with everyone: my roommates, my boyfriend, random people on the street. I officially worked in radio! I was a disc jockey. And the transcripts, the university, and my plans for teaching just moved to the back burner. The timing was perfect as we were looking for a reason to throw another party.

I was hired for weekend overnights, which made sense as I had zero radio experience. I was so thrilled to be working at this radio station, I needed to constantly be pinched to make sure I wasn't dreaming. I still lived in my house on campus, but gladly drove the 3 hour round trip commute to my new job.

I still continued to wait tables. Part time radio gigs don't pay the rent, but I gladly gave my shifts away for any opportunity to be on the air.

I was so nervous at first. I was talking on the radio, and hundreds, and thousands of people were going to hear me. What if I freaked out? In the early days Warren would drive with me, and he'd sit in the car the entire time listening to my show. Knowing he was nearby made it a little less scary. (Don't tell me you can't find Mr. Right while doing a keg stand.)

Things at the station were about to move at rapid speed. I was working an early morning shift on a Saturday just a few weeks into my employment. I remember thinking that I was awful that day. I thought that everything coming out of my mouth was terrible. This was especially troubling because Greg was working the shift after me. I envisioned him driving in and listening to this giant suck-fest wondering why he hired me in the first place. The end of my show was approaching when Greg walked into the studio and sat in a chair. Things just felt weird. He clearly had something on his mind and was getting ready to say something to me.

So this was it. My radio experience was coming to an end. It's been fun, teaching here I come. Then Greg offered me the full-time overnight position. It turns out I didn't suck! He liked me, and wanted to give me a bigger role. Just a month or so after being hired, I was officially a full time radio personality! He told me that I was extremely talented, and had enormous potential. Those words from Greg meant more than the job itself. This would be the first of many promotions over the course of my first year in radio.

After barely settling into the overnight position, I was once again promoted. I was moved to the 7 p.m. to midnight shift, making me the new full time "night jock". I don't think the move came with a pay increase, but it didn't matter. This wasn't about money. I was just over the moon that they considered me skilled enough for the time slot. Now I was on when people could hear me! Lots more people. I was growing more confident every day and really developing as a radio personality. I was enjoying my role as the night jock and was getting great feedback.

I was getting that feedback not just from my boss, but from his bosses too, the owners of the station. I was still walking on air every day over my good fortune. I was working for this legendary program director at a really cool radio station. It just didn't seem real. So when Greg wanted to talk to me again, it couldn't be good news, I'd had too much of that in such a short amount of time already.

Was this where I pay the piper?

Greg was moving me again, this time to middays. The higher ups had a meeting and decided that I would be better in that position than the current host. But she was a "real" DJ, she was so well known, they really thought I could replace her? Feeling flattered was an understatement; this promotion was a HUGE move! I would be on smack dab in the middle of the day. If lots of people can hear you from seven to midnight then everyone can hear you from 10 a.m. to 2 p.m.

My career was taking off. I HAD a career, and my future looked bright. But for as amazing as this third promotion was, it would not be the last. Before the year was up, I was made the host of the morning show. This is the most important on-air position on the radio. I could give you a hundred reasons why promotions like this just don't happen, but the impossible sometimes happens. And it had just happened to me. Even though I had the support and respect of my boss and mentor, other forces had to be involved. Surely my guardian angels were showing me some serious love. I was the morning show host at a popular radio station in the state capitol just one year after graduating from broadcast arts school.

I don't know what I did to get so lucky, but I was going to make sure to pay it forward for as long as possible.

There would be some major changes at the radio station around this time, including the fact that Greg was leaving. He had encouraged me so much and played such an important role in my journey that his leaving caused a major void. But I was grateful for all he'd done for me, and I was determined to make him proud.

There were a lot of things about this new morning show that were highly unusual. The first one was that the host, me, had less than a year of radio experience. But it was also one of the only all-girl morning shows to probably ever exist. Yep, this morning show was going to be me and another girl, just the two of us.

Sisters were doing it for themselves.

My new partner was a college student who was doing an internship at the radio station. She and I had become fast friends over the past few months, and when one of the station owners noticed the "chemistry" between us, the plan was put in motion. We were two young girls who had very little experience going up against REAL morning shows. Some had been broadcasting for decades.

It doesn't sound like this is going to end well, but sure enough we made our mark in the morning! Over the next year, our girl morning show climbed in the ratings, and we developed a fan base even we couldn't have realized. Our show would come to an end after a years time, but not because we didn't succeed. We heard from every corner of the city. People were letting us know what our show meant to them, and thanking us for the ride. I learned that I could touch people through the radio in a way I never fathomed.

What started from a love for music, now became a way to not just entertain, but to uplift and make a difference.

The revelation may have come too late, though. I had moved so fast through this radio station, moving up and moving up. But suddenly I was making the decision to move out, leaving the show and the station I loved so much. I was walking away, possibly forever. It didn't make sense to anyone. Why would I leave something I worked so hard for? And possibly rethink my career altogether?

I would learn a few more lessons about radio and myself too. I might not be cut out for this profession, regardless of how much I wanted it.

Leaving now was my choice, but maybe the FINAL decision wasn't in my hands at all. If you believe in destiny and fate then you know you're only partly in control.

And destiny thought it was cute that I was thinking "teacher" again.

Chapter Five

YOU REALLY HAVE TO LOVE SOMETHING TO LET IT MAKE YOU FAT

As amazing as that first year at the station was, the second year would be the complete and polar opposite. I would go from constant promotions and accolades to a hard dose of reality. And fast.

I was feeling incredibly positive in my role as morning show host, and met the challenge head on. After all, this type of opportunity didn't happen to young girls fresh out of broadcast school. I was proud of myself and was going to prove to everyone just what I could do! The odds seemed to be stacked against a show lead by a girl with just one year of radio experience and another girl, who was an intern prior to being bumped up to co-host. There's no way these two girls could pull this off. There were serious morning shows in this city, shows that had been a part of the radio landscape for decades. Would we be laughed off the air? What kind of crazy experiment was this? The two of us worked hard and were determined to make the most of this miraculous opportunity. We were two girls in the morning, ready to take on the world! We had no real assistance in making this show work. We had no prep services, no news services, no AP wire, none of the things most all morning shows rely on to perform every morning.

My partner actually picked up newspapers on her way in every morning and would cut stories out of the paper for her newscasts. We had four hours to fill every morning and it was up to us to figure out how to do that. So between us we developed bench mark features, regular segments, goofy and engaging contests, and it was working. We were connecting with the morning audience.

People were tuning in daily for "The Melrose Place update" set to cheesy soap opera music, and "Allyson the hypochondriac," a contest for prizes. Real quality stuff. Not only were we gaining popularity, we were also gaining ratings. And we found ourselves moving right to the top of the ranks! We were even contending with the heritage morning show in the city, the show that had been number one for decades. This just doesn't happen.

We were featured in magazines, in the local newspapers; we hosted the local portion of Jerry Lewis' MDA telethon, and got a ton of television attention when we walked from Lansing to Detroit for charity. It was a stunt that was born after I got lost walking back to the radio station from the mall. We were using our everyday experiences to come up with material for our show, and we were doing it all by ourselves.

So how could this be anything but a happy time? Why was I thinking about walking away?

For as much of an asset as this morning show proved to be, I wasn't receiving the respect or gratitude that you'd expect for a job well done. I was working for seven dollars an hour. You did hear that right, I was hosting a morning show for seven large an hour. My partner made a whopping six dollars an hour. I recall standing on the sidewalk one day and looking up the street at a sandwich board sign promoting nine dollars an hour to work at the fast food restaurant behind the sign. That eye opening moment was not lost on me. But I was patient and I didn't mind paying my dues. I've never minded that.

But when the dues have been paid, do right by me, because it's the right thing to do.

I was learning that some people in this industry believed that their "professional position" allowed them to take breaks from human decency. "Well that's radio," was the battle cry, as if somehow certain professions or titles come with free passes from good behavior. For the record, there is no job title in life that allows that. You are required to be decent and to treat people fairly. Always. My low salary was actually the least of my worries, albeit still an issue. Interestingly enough, I was paying seven dollars a day, every day, to park my car in the garage next to the radio station, so half of my monthly salary went to parking my car.

As I said, it wasn't the low pay that had me looking to leave, it was the disrespect and negative atmosphere that was getting to me. It wasn't a nurturing environment. None of the people around me, specifically above me, were placing any value on me as a worker, or crediting me for the successful show that I was delivering. I didn't need pats on the back or foot massages, but I wanted respect. I wanted to be valued. I had earned that.

But that wasn't going to happen.

When I became host of the morning show, I finally moved from my campus house to be closer to the radio station. My show started much too early in the morning for a ninety minute, one way commute to be added to the mix. So here I was in a new city, an hour and a half away from all of my friends, and my social life, and I was feeling very isolated. The radio station had become the center of my life, and when things started to go south there I started to withdraw.

My boyfriend made the decision to move with me when I finally had to relocate. We had been together for two years and didn't want that much distance between us. We were into each other. So we packed up our minimal belongings at our college houses, said goodbye to our roommates and headed to Lansing. He was still a student, and needed to keep his job at the local pizza place on campus. Now it was his turn to make the ninety minute commute. Sure he could have found a "pizza guy" job closer to our new home, but he had seniority there, and he knew how to make the secret sauce. (That's huge, you don't walk away from that.)

I was already feeling disconnected from the radio station, and far away from my friends in an unfamiliar city. Now I didn't see Warren almost at all. My workday would end around one or two in the afternoon. Warren would leave for his job everyday around three. So we literally had about an hour a day to spend together. He'd come home from work after midnight, just a few hours before I'd wake up for my 5 a.m. morning show. We couldn't have been on more opposite ends of the day, and I felt very alone.

I was having conflicting feelings of absolutely loving my job, and my show, but struggling with the negativity I had recently encountered. I was not being respected or appreciated. I was being overlooked and taken advantage of. And I'd had the eye opening realization that being a female was going to make this career path even harder.

And it wasn't just about being a female, but being a "larger" female. There's very little room, no pun intended, for overweight women in the entertainment industry. "You gotta' lot of nerve there girly, walking around NOT being perfect. Don't you think you'd be more comfortable staying completely out of view?"

Now no one is going to actually make that comment out loud, but it's pretty much the wide spread sentiment.

It turns out, feeling sad and being alone can lead to extreme eating! That's really the only way to explain the eating that I did that year. Something I learned about myself at that time? I'm a "feelings" eater.

And boy was I filled with feelings.

Food became my friend, my social life, my mood lifting drug. I was eating non-stop. You know you have a problem when your checks to the pizza place across town are bouncing and the brothers pictured on the box are coming to your apartment to shake you down.

Since Warren and I were keeping opposite schedules, neither of us were really noticing the weight gain. It was also partly because I had started wearing those black stretchy pants. This would prove to be a hazardous move as a person can continue to grow in those things without realizing what is happening.

What was happening was I was packing on some serious "sad" pounds, and by the time I left the radio station I was seventy pounds heavier. I had gained all of that weight in less than a year, and it was the final reason that gave me the courage to leave my job. I had become very overweight, I was making no money, and I was miserable all the time.

How could things have changed so drastically in just a years time?

Everything had been amazing, my career was blossoming, and now I was rethinking everything. Maybe radio wasn't for me after all. I wasn't cut out for the "cut-throat" side of the business.

So, on a random Monday in April, after finishing my morning show, I walked down to the program directors office and put in my two weeks notice. He was stunned. People don't walk away from hosting popular morning shows. To be honest, I don't think he really believed I was serious. I think he thought I was blowing off steam. But I meant it, and a weight was lifted off of my soul as soon as I said the words.

Unfortunately the weight that had accumulated on my ass stayed put.

I was told that I would never work in radio again. I guess attempting to make me feel bad seemed like a good tactic in making me change my mind instead of offering me more money or showing me respect, which actually might have worked. It solidified what I knew in my heart already, that leaving was the right thing to do. I tried my best to honor the two weeks' notice I had given, but I only made it to the following Wednesday, two days shy. That would have to be good enough. I finished my last show, turned in my key, and drove my car out of the insanely expensive parking garage for the last time.

I wasn't looking back, I was now looking forward. I needed to get healthy and happy again. And if it meant putting radio behind me, I was prepared to do that.

Right around this time Warren finally noticed the weight gain, and he agreed that we would put the blame on the black stretchy pants.

I felt bad leaving the audience I had come to love, and I felt bad leaving my morning show partner. Despite the stress coming between us at times, we were friends. And we kept in touch after I left. They paired her with a new host and I knew that she would be okay. How much of an impact our morning show had made in that year soon became very apparent.

After I left, the mail came in like crazy. It was pre-internet, so people had to make their feelings known through stamped envelopes. I remember her coming to my apartment with this large postal box filled to the top with letters. So many letters. It was truly remarkable. I knew people enjoyed our show but I hadn't realized to what degree. We had really connected with the audience, and they were sad the girl show was gone.

I read letters from so many different people: women AND men, moms and dads, college professors, doctors, truck drivers, students and grandmas. Grandmas were listening to an alternative radio station? I guess if the morning show is good enough it doesn't matter what type of music is playing. I had connected with people through the radio, even helped people through hard times, and that meant the world to me. But this show business side, the heartless side, I just wasn't prepared to handle that.

I contacted the university I had planned to attend before broadcast school and enrolled for fall semester. In September I would be back in school, and back on track to become a teacher. In the meantime, I started working on the weight. Warren and I started walking all over the city, miles and miles every day. And there weren't any more orders to the pizza place, though we were square on any outstanding checks.

I was getting healthy and working my way back to the happy person I was when I started this crazy radio ride. Spring turned to summer, and life was getting back on track. We were getting ready to move back home, near the university, and excited about the future. I lost forty pounds and was not only physically stronger, but mentally and emotionally too. And my radio experience was fading in the rear view mirror. I still felt sadness over walking away from something that seemed so “meant to be”.

My life was moving in a different direction, but it looked like radio wasn’t done with me yet. That July I learned that a brand new alternative station was launching in Detroit. This format was gaining steam and more of these stations were popping up around the country, including a second one in Detroit. And there was more, this new station employed some friendly faces from my past. Greg was there! He was hosting the mid-day show. Another friend from the old radio station was there too, hosting the night show. Both of these people had been part of my positive journey that first year in radio, and here they were at this new station in Detroit; a radio station still in the process of hiring. My brain was telling me to ignore all of this, but my heart was telling me to give it one more try.

It was really hard ignoring the “signs”. I’m a signs girl! I’m an “Everything happens for a reason,” girl, and surely the universe was gently nudging me back to the radio. My friends were there, my mentor was there, and a second radio station that played the music I loved was launching and needed staff. These were absolutely signs that this was meant to be. And what could it hurt to try? I was already enrolled for fall semester at the university, so rolling the dice on this possible radio job couldn’t derail those plans.

I went for it.

I put together a demo tape and with my very limited resume, dropped them in a Fed-Ex envelope and overnighted it to Detroit. It was a shot in the dark, a serious long shot. Detroit was the sixth largest market in the country. That is big time! Radio stations in this city employ seasoned and talented radio pros. So while I remained hopeful, I stayed realistic.

On a random Thursday morning, Warren and I went to the post office to spend one of our last twenty dollar bills on shipping this package.

Then we jumped in our car and headed out of town. We were off on a long weekend of visiting friends and looking for apartments for the fall. We were completely unaware that by the time this weekend was over life would change drastically again.

Fate and destiny move quickly, and that would be apparent by the red flashing light on the answering machine that caught our attention when we came home late that Sunday night.

Chapter Six

THEY MAKE A TEA FOR THAT?

It was peculiar to find a message on our answering machine when we returned home on Sunday night, mostly because we had just spent the past four days with everyone we knew. Our friends and family knew that we were back at our old stomping grounds looking for apartments. We didn't really have friends in this new city we lived in, and we didn't get many calls to begin with. So when we noticed the flashing message light we determined it was either a wrong number or a telemarketer. Because we were exhausted from our weekend, the long drive home, and it being so late, the decision was almost made to NOT press play at that moment. But my OCD wasn't going to allow a light to continue to flash all night long, so for that reason alone I hit play.

And I couldn't believe my ears when the message began; it was the Music Director from the Detroit radio station.

The Detroit radio station I had JUST sent my resume to on Thursday? They were calling me? Already? How? It was only this past Thursday that I overnighted my package, how could they be calling me so soon? This message was left on my machine Friday afternoon, meaning they called me the day they received it. I was astounded.

The very definition of astounded!

Here it was after midnight on Sunday and I was listening to this man invite me to meet with them on Monday.

Wait, tomorrow Monday? What is happening?

Even as I recall it, it still doesn't seem real. Once again, these things just do not happen! What should have happened was for my tape and resume to be received, sit on a pile of others for a week—possibly longer, then opened, looked at and listened to, then cast aside due to lack of major market experience, or much experience period. Instead, what I never could have imagined, EVER, had happened, was happening; that on the very day they received my information, they immediately called me back to set up an appointment to meet for the very next business day.

Well wham, bam, and thank you ma'am!

It's the middle of the night on Sunday, so technically it's Monday already, and this long shot has just paid off! Radio has come flooding back into my life at rapid speed.

In a matter of hours I'd be in Detroit, the sixth largest market in the country, talking with important people about possibly working at this radio station. The odds that I was going to get any sleep that night were slim as I was bouncing off the walls at this point.

What would I wear? Would my hair be perfect? What would I say? Did we even have gas money for me to get to Detroit?

There were so many questions. I did manage to get a little bit of sleep, although I tossed and turned for most of what was left of the night. I needed to be up bright and early so I could place a phone call the second the business day began, and RSVP an enthusiastic "ABSOLUTELY" at the request to meet today.

The sun was up, and whether or not I'd gotten adequate rest was irrelevant, as there was enough adrenaline pumping through me to equal twenty cups of coffee.

I sat by the phone with my eyes keenly focused on the clock, and the second it struck 9 a.m. I picked it up and began dialing. In my head, I was envisioning a scene out of a movie, a high rise building in a busy city, with hundreds of people in suits and dresses milling about desks, talking on phones, and conducting high level entertainment business.

And I was calling this important place. Just thinking about it made me woozy.

A voice on the other end of the phone placed me on hold while she located the Music Director whose call I was returning. Then in mere moments, he was on the phone, and I was talking to him. He had probably just been on another line, with Simon Le Bon, talking on one of those fancy phone headsets. And now he was talking to me. This was the story playing out in my head; this is how big of a deal this was.

He told me they were impressed with what I sent and asked if I could come to the station that afternoon for an interview? A definitive "Yes," came through my cracking voice, and a plan to meet in a few hours was sealed. There was so much to do now, I had to get ready. It was time to get fabulous—big city fabulous! Then just as I was making my way from the telephone, it rang. I had just hung it up and now it was ringing.

Oh no, did they change their mind?

It was in fact the Music Director calling back, but not because they'd changed their mind, he just had one more important detail for me.

"We'll need you to take a drug test when you get here. That won't be a problem will it?"

"Absolutely not," I responded.

"Good, then we'll see you soon."

Click.

This absolutely WAS going to be a problem!

Now to be clear, I was still in college, and still attending college parties. At these parties there may have been peculiar smoke swirling around me, not that I ever inhaled personally. (Didn't that work for a President?) So in the event that this "contact" smoke seeped, against my will, into my system, then it was possible it could cause me to fail a drug test.

Seriously?

My dreams were about to go up in smoke, literally. I learned from friends who smoked, who were tested for work, that there was a tea available for purchase from the big box nutrition store. Drinking the tea would cause an all clear result, and I would pass this test with flying colors. I couldn't let youthful indiscretions cost me this huge opportunity, so off to the mall I went, to buy tea.

What a bizarre day this was going to be.

I was already pressed for time, and now I was in my kitchen reading the back of this box so I could follow the instructions to a tee. I continued getting ready for my meeting, primping and preening, while the tea boiled on the stove. Before long it was time to go. I was already looking at an hour and a half commute, and now, newly added to the itinerary, was drinking a gallon of tea. And I'd have to drink it for the entire duration of the drive into the city.

I did not envy my bladder.

I filled up all the cups I could find in my kitchen and put them in the front seat with me, and as I made my way down the expressway, I chugged tea. And chugged some more.

I had driven about a half hour without the need for a potty break, but the urge to go finally set in. Soon I was hitting almost every exit, to stop and use various restaurant bathrooms, for the remainder of the commute.

Well, if I didn't get this job maybe I could write a travel guide on the best rest rooms along I-96 East.

I finally arrived at my destination and it was as magical as I envisioned during the initial phone call. This building WAS right out of the movies. It was, it IS, majestic. I was in the Fisher Building. It's actually considered "living art." The marble, the brass, the tiles—I couldn't stop staring straight up at the ceilings as I walked. Even with the possibility of tripping and breaking something, I couldn't keep my eyes in front of me. I was drinking in every square inch of this gorgeous historical building in the center of Detroit.

My interview was here? I could possibly work here?

It was intoxicating. And the beauty didn't end in the lobby of this building, as there was so much more to see. I took the elevators up to the radio station which occupied the 21st, 22nd, and 23rd floors. I was going to the very top of the building, and the views were spectacular.

I was Alice and this was Wonderland.

I let the receptionist know I was there for an interview, and then waited to see what other amazing things were in store for me. It turned out my meeting would not be with the Music Director I'd spoken to on the phone. I was meeting the Program Director, the boss, the big wig! And this Program Director, PD for short, was that and more. He was legendary, IS legendary, as he is still very well-known and respected. People know who he is, and I was about to meet him.

My grandma must have gotten some high level position in heaven where she controls the strings, because there had to be so much more at play here. This was like a dream, thank you Grandma.

I was led into his office and waited for what seemed like forever, (but nerves will cause those feelings). In came this larger than life person, just bursting with energy and enthusiasm, and very nice. I felt comfortable immediately, and we just started talking. We talked about my radio experience and my career goals, and we talked about the new direction he was taking this station. It was already one of the most successful CHR stations in the country and now he was gambling on this popular new alternative format.

As we continued to talk, he started handing me paperwork to

sign, and it became clear that this was not an interview. I was being hired right there on the spot. I assumed that we'd talk, the way you do in an interview, and at the conclusion I'd hear, "Well thanks for coming in, we'll let you know our decision in a few days." And that alone would have been good enough for me. But I wasn't going to need to wait. As I sat there in his office, at that moment, I was being hired.

I just needed to stay cool and not freak out.

Because when the realization hit that I officially worked at this radio station, in this beautiful building, in this amazing city of Detroit, Market #6, a circus, a parade, and fifteen marching bands proceeded to simultaneously happen inside my body.

I walked into his office with a dream, and I was walking out a part of the team. The impossible had happened again. There was still the issue of the drug test, and it was the funniest part. When our meeting concluded, he brought up the uncomfortable topic of "the test", and made his feelings pretty clear.

He proceeded to tell me that if I didn't think I could pass to come clean now, and we would reschedule the test. If I failed it he would not be able to hire me at all, so he'd rather me be up-front with him, and then I could take it at a more "passable" time.

I laughed to myself as I thought, "This would have been great information to have when I started this day."

I decided to put my trust in the tea. I also didn't want my new boss to know that I sometimes come in contact with other people's smoke, so off to take the test I went. I had made so many trips to the bathroom en route to this meeting, that now when it was time to deliver a sample, I was plumb out! The results came back inconclusive due to not having enough to test. And inconclusive was good enough, I passed!

The last piece of the puzzle popped into place, and on that 13th day of July, I became an employee at the radio station I would call home for the next twenty years. And what an amazing ride it would be.

I immediately dropped my classes for fall semester at the university, as it was now evident now that radio was truly my destiny.

Chapter Seven

THEY CALLED IT "BLACK MONDAY"

It was almost September and our lease was up in Lansing, so we could finally move back home. My boyfriend was still a student at the university and still the number one pizza delivery guy. I mean he was delivering pizzas to future Detroit Lions quarterbacks and the managers of very famous Motor City rockers, so yeah, he was a big deal!

Living near the university was still the plan, so we moved into a cute little apartment surrounded by ponds and wildlife, and the commute from my front door to Detroit was 30 minutes. It was good to be home again.

I wasn't working at my new radio station often, but just being employed there was a high. For the first couple of months I worked the Friday overnight, and it was my only shift. This station had a large staff, with many on-air personalities, and many "famous" on air personalities. I couldn't believe that I was working with some of these people.

As exciting as it was just to be a part of it, working only the Friday overnight made me feel invisible, but I was determined to make the hours that I was on the air count. It was an intimidating fact that so many talented jocks dominated these airwaves, so many well-known broadcasters, with so few time slots available.

Two months in I still hadn't met the majority of the staff. I'd see the person that came on before me, and the person that came on after, but that was pretty much the extent of my interaction with my co-workers. But I was driven and I never got discouraged. So what if every famous DJ on the planet worked at this radio station? It didn't mean that I couldn't shine too. Opportunities surround us all the time. We just have to be open and ready for them.

It would have been easy for me to feel shadowed by these towering broadcast figures, but if I believed I belonged here, then they would too. I was on the air in the city of Detroit. Whether it was in the middle of the night or not, a million people might be tuning in, and I was bowled over by the thought.

I got my first bump up when I was scheduled to work a Saturday morning. This was more exposure than the Friday overnights. How many people were up and running errands, driving around the city, working, doing whatever they do, while listening to me? I couldn't let my nerves get the best of me. "Just act like you're talking to ONE person and you'll be fine."

This was the first time I saw daylight shine through those studio windows and I was nervous and excited all at once. I had to be perfect! This was serious, these were daytime hours. If that wasn't exciting enough, I received a call from my PD during my first show.

There's a bit of panic that washes over when you see the studio "hot line" ring. The hot line is the emergency line, the boss line. It not only flashes on the phone but usually causes lights to flash in the studio. Generally you don't like to see it ring.

Oh no, was I blowing it?

Quite the contrary, it was my boss calling, but he had nothing but good things to say. He was golfing with friends, probably very important friends, and they were listening. He just wanted to call to say that I sounded great and to keep up the good work. Well you can keep this week's check and knock me over with a feather—that phone call motivated me beyond words. I was on his radar, he was happy with my performance, and I was working while the sun was up.

Good things were happening.

Summer turned into fall, fall turned into winter, and I was working more and more as time went on. I even picked up quite a few shifts over the holidays while the full-timers took their vacations. Detroit was getting to know Allyson, and I was feeling comfortable and at-home at this radio station. I felt like I belonged here.

In January I received a call at home from the station. There was a mandatory meeting that everyone needed to attend. It was ominous, but exciting—my first meeting! I was actually going to be in the same room with the entire radio station staff for the first time! Hopefully this positive feeling would continue.

What could be happening that required everyone's presence, though?

It wouldn't be long before we had our answer to that. Everyone congregated in the conference room on the 23rd floor, and there I was, in this room with every single person who worked here. There were some big deal radio people in this room, and with these giant picture windows highlighting every view of the city, I was feeling like I was in a movie again.

Before long the PD entered the room. The man who brought me on board was about to address the crowd and you could have heard a pin drop. He was in really great spirits, so it was hard at first to make out that the news he was relaying wasn't good news at all. Through a detailed and entertaining story, he was telling us that he was leaving.

I couldn't tell if it was by his choice or not, but I suspected that it wasn't. This larger than life, legendary radio God was leaving? But we were just getting started.

I was just getting started.

The plan to flip the station from Top 40 to Alternative was still in progress, and from what I could tell this was all his vision. How could he be leaving?

And what would that mean for the rest of us? It was hard to wrap my brain around it. And just six months into my new journey, the man who called me back to the radio was no more. It happened that quickly. Within days of the meeting he was gone, and whether or not I would still have a place there remained uncertain.

I knew this much though, I had made the decision on the day I was hired that if I was giving radio a second chance, I was in it for the long haul. There was no more Plan B. I was committed to this career and whatever happened next, I would meet it head on.

At first nothing changed, and we continued on as normal. I was even getting to know my co-workers better. One of my new friends at work was Darren. Darren was famous, he was a big deal. I used to listen to him on the radio all the time, back when radio was just something I dreamt about, and I'd imagine actually working with him some day. Later in life I'd learn about the "law of attraction", but it turns out long before I knew what it was, I had been applying it to my life.

Here I was actually working with Darren, the way I envisioned years earlier. I guess that stuff really works. Darren and I were about to share a crazy radio experience that no one could have predicted, so I was glad we had become such good friends.

In time the vacated Program Director position had been filled, a replacement was named and we would soon be meeting our new boss. It was exciting and scary at the same time. The Program Director is the decider, the visionary, the shot caller. It is their job to create a successful radio station, so they are given the tools, support, and authority to do whatever they need to do to implement their goals.

I needed to keep the faith that I would fit into the new guy's vision. This would be my third boss. I'd been lucky twice before, with both of my PD's seeing value in me.

Is the third time the charm? Or would it be three strikes and you're out?

Soon I'd find out if three was my lucky number when word came that it was time for us to meet. A new chapter was about to begin at this radio station, but there was no way to know exactly how NEW it would be. Everyone was anxious at the arrival of our new leader, who was brought in to make things happen, to take this station to the next level, and that was going to affect all of us. We just didn't know to what degree yet.

The day came for me to meet my new boss, and it felt like a job interview all over again, which I guess, technically, it was. I needed him to like me—I needed him to like me a lot. Not only was I attempting to keep the job I already had, but there was potential now for a bigger role at the radio station. Depending on how talented and valuable he considered me, he could possibly promote me, or he might not want me at all.

There was a lot at stake.

I got myself cool, calm, and collected, and I was off to our meeting. I liked him right away, and it felt mutual. He was very friendly, and I felt comfortable talking to him. He was passionate about this music and this format, and he could tell through our conversation that I was, too.

At this period of time, alternative music was huge. It was the era of Nirvana, Pearl Jam, Nine Inch Nails, Janes Addiction, and many others, and the people who worked at these radio stations really lived the lifestyle. It was all about the music, and it was about making a statement, and being non-conformist. These bands and their fans were forging their own path, and that kind of spoke to me. I liked the idea of not having to all be the same and live the same and do the same thing. We could be different and be appreciated for it, and even though I'm not as into the music as before, that message is still important to me. At that time I fully embraced the music and lifestyle though, down to the clothes.

It was an important to have these attributes, and at this time in my life I had them. I even dressed the part in my cut off jean shorts over black tights, concert tee-shirts, and Doc Marten boots.

I know what you're thinking—very hot.

I could tell it was important to the new PD that whoever was going to work for him needed to be authentic in their attitude and approach, and I left the interview feeling that I definitely had passed the test.

I felt good about our meeting, but now it was just time to wait as he continued to have these meetings with the other members of the staff. What exactly I was waiting for I wasn't sure, but there was just this feeling in the air that there would be more to come. I just had no idea how drastic the "more to come" was about to be. A shakeup was eminent, and on a Monday not long after these meetings, everyone received a call to come in again. And one by one, every single on air personality was let go.

The afternoon host was retained. He was one of Detroit's top personalities, but he was moved to a different time slot. By the end of the day the rest of the entire on air lineup was gone.

Everyone—gone.

This was a radio station without DJ's.

Darren and I were also called in that day, but we received different information. We had made the cut, and were the only other two to survive.

It was hard to feel excited when so many people had just lost their jobs that day. There was a sense of elation though, knowing that a brand new team was going to be assembled, and I was being kept to be part of that.

Radio is tough, and that was a tough day.

Some seriously talented and well know broadcasters were released on "Black Monday", and as of this moment just Darren and I were moving forward. If you can be mournful and excited at the same time, then I was. Really big things were coming and I was chosen to be a part of them. I had just come dangerously close to a swinging ax that took out some amazingly talented people, and I avoided being cut.

Yep, I'd say this radio thing was meant to be.

Chapter Eight

IT'S A SMALL WORLD AFTER ALL

Eight months after leaving my first radio job, with thoughts of leaving radio altogether, I was working at my dream radio station in Detroit, the 6th largest market in the country. Detroit would eventually drop to market twelve in the coming years, but at this moment there were only five markets bigger. Detroit was big time, Detroit IS big time! Not only had I attained the unimaginable dream of working here, I had just survived one of the largest firings I'd experience in my career. And Darren and I were the only ones left.

It was hard to wrap my brain around all that had happened, or comprehend everything that was about to unfold. Radio stations provide 24 hour a day programming, and this station currently had no staff, how was this going to work? One immediate change was how much I was about to work. I went from working once, maybe twice a weekend, to working every single day, seven days a week, with no days off. And that was fine with me. My increased hours didn't mean I was being heard more though, in fact it was quite the opposite, I wasn't being heard at all now.

Radio stations commonly engage the audience in what is called "stunting", and it's exactly what it sounds like, performing stunts to capture the audience's attention. Stunting usually takes place when a brand new radio station is being launched, or an existing station is about to re-launch or flip formats.

My radio station was in the middle of a re-launch. Regular listeners tuning in expecting to hear familiar voices found all of the on-air personalities had vanished. The familiar music stayed the same, and recorded promos informed the audience that the DJ's had been sent to DJ camp so they could get better, and when they returned they'd be so good they may even sound like different people.

I'm sure the fired DJs did not appreciate this, but as far as stunting goes it was pretty clever.

For weeks and weeks, the city of Detroit continued to hear about this entire lineup of on air personalities who'd been sent off to DJ camp and the listener's interest definitely piqued.

What was going on at this radio station? What were the DJ's going to sound like when they returned?

Back at the station Darren and I were working non-stop running the board, which means we were pushing buttons and keeping the music, commercials, and all other content on the air. We weren't doing any broadcasting though, as I suppose we were technically "at DJ camp" too. My imagination was running wild at this time, trying to speculate just what my role would be at this new station. I had been kept on staff, so surely this meant I would be a part of the new on air lineup. Darren and I would muse about our possible new air shifts. Would he be the new afternoon guy? Would I be the new midday girl? What else could possibly happen? We were clearly kept for a reason, and I was so sure that something big was on the horizon, for both of us. (Slow your roll there girl, don't go putting carts in front of horses, or all the eggs in one basket. Insert applicable old timey saying here.)

The day finally arrived and the DJs came back from camp, the stunting was over, and a brand new on-air staff was unveiled. Interviews and hiring had taken place throughout the weeks of stunting, and an entire team had been assembled. From top to bottom, every single air shift had been filled. There was a new morning show, new midday, afternoon and night personalities, and an overnight jock too. Alas, Darren and I had not been considered for any of those positions. We would go back to our part time roles, and our regular air shifts. It was bittersweet as my daydreaming had gotten the best of me. Even though there was no full time job, I still worked there, and I'd been able to make a nice chunk of cash over the past several weeks, too! My radio guardian angel had been good to me so far, maybe expecting a prime shift in such a large market only eight months after being hired was a little too much to hope for. I was excited to be a part of this brand new station and the future seemed promising.

Right off the bat I was asked to sit in with the new morning host. He needed a cohost as the rest of his team hadn't arrived in Detroit yet. This was huge! I was being asked to do mornings! Even if it was just for a day or two it was a big deal. And when my short term assignment came to an end, my new boss heaped a lot of praise on me. He was impressed with my performance, and encouraged me to be patient—when there was an opening he'd promote me.

Words like this are equivalent to gold.

In the radio, television, & entertainment industry, it can be hard to make your mark, and some people never do. It's the luck of the draw sometimes, even for people with immense talent, so just the promise of something more can sustain you for a long time. I had impressed my new boss, and he seemed to like me a lot. That was enough for me at the time.

The new staff all became very close right out of the gate. It was really a tight knit group of people, and even though Darren and I joked that we were stepchildren from a previous marriage, the atmosphere was positive. Something else happened that was extremely positive; a merger had recently taken place, making me an employee of ABC/Disney. This company now owned my radio station.

I officially worked for ABC/Disney!

One of my prized possessions, that I still carry to this day, is my ABC I.D. card. (My picture and the ABC logo on a driver's license style card.) I always looked forward to having to produce two forms of ID because I sure loved showing that card to people. And working for Disney was pretty amazing. We got free passes to the park that came in Christmas cards from Michael Eisner, 35% off at the Disney Store, a silver card that allowed you 24 visits a year to all the parks for you and three guests—and these were just some of the perks.

Of course, living in Michigan made it hard to take full advantage of these perks, but just having them was exciting. My life had changed quite a bit in that last year, and even though I still only worked part time I felt on top of the world.

The radio station was taking off too!

We rode floats in the Detroit Thanksgiving Day Parade, we starred in TV commercials, we were featured in the previews at movie theaters, and we threw some of the biggest concerts in town. I could start any random work day riding the elevator up with Barry Sanders and ending my day taking the elevator down with Kid Rock. As far as experiences go, I was having unbelievable ones, but I did long for more in my career. And after about a year I would finally get the bump to full time. The female sidekick was leaving the morning show, and my boss was moving the overnight girl into her spot, leaving overnights available.

Now an impatient person might have become cranky at being overlooked for the morning show position, especially since she made such a splash filling in as co-host those first few days. Thankfully, I'm a patient person, and although I may silently question people's judgement, I'm happy to pay my dues and wait my turn. So I wasn't going to get the morning show job, that clearly wasn't my "meant to be." But I was being promoted to full time overnights, and I was about to sign my first ever contract.

What an amazing feeling! I was signing a contract! That's what real entertainment professionals do, they have "people", and they sign "deals." Well I didn't have "people" yet, but I was about to sign a deal. I was about to get benefits. I was about to get a salary. And I'll never forget that magical experience.

I met with our General Manager in his office on the 23rd floor of the Fisher Building. He was sitting at his desk, which I'm sure was made of the finest wood and leather, and I sat on the other side. We were face to face. I was doing everything I could not to throw up everywhere, because what a mood killer that would be! Then he handed me a contract.

My contract!

In my hands I held my first contract, and it was stunning. I was looking at 20 to 30 pieces of paper stapled together, with important legal words written on them, outlining my next 5 years of employment. I was signing a 5 year deal! This is what TV stars and sports figures do, they sign multi-year deals.

And as I looked at this stack of papers stapled together, with my eyes as wide as silver dollars, the General Manager had one more thing for me. He reached into his desk and pulled out a beautiful Mickey Mouse pen in a decorative case and handed it to me. I was going to sign my first contract, to work for ABC/Disney, with this fancy limited edition pen.

And at that moment, I figured my GM wouldn't mind if a little bit of water fell from my eyes. I took the pen out of the box and signed my contract right then and there.

By the time I left that office I was a full time employee—a full time member of the air staff. I still keep that Mickey Mouse pen in the beautiful decorative box with my most important treasures. My official major market journey began with the stroke of that pen.

Chapter Nine

PATIENCE IS A VIRTUE, AINT THAT THE TRUTH?

The next five years were a whirlwind and a standstill all at once. It's a funny thing about time and the perspective that it gives you. When I was in the thick of it, living it, I was filled with such frustration over the snail's pace my career was moving. Amazing things were happening daily yet I was so desperate to get "there."

At this point I knew with every fiber of my being that I was meant to make my mark on this industry, to be "someone", and that everything that had happened in my life so far was preparing me for something big, for something great. I knew that it was (here comes the corniness) written in the stars. Outside forces weren't just pushing me along this path, they were making sure I stayed on it, and that couldn't be denied. But many more years would go by before my career would get to the next level, and there would be a lot of rejection in my future.

In hindsight, rejection can actually be a wonderful thing. It's just impossible to make sense of that as it's happening. My patience and my belief that this was what I was supposed to be doing kept me from reacting to the numerous times I would be denied in the years to come. No good comes from cutting off your nose to spite your face, right? But simultaneously I was experiencing serious professional highs too, of pretty epic proportions.

We're all fans of someone; we know what it feels like to have a favorite movie star, a favorite TV star, a favorite rock star. Maybe we've even been members of a fan club, like when I was nine years old and belonged to the Barry Manilow fan club. I got the official monthly newsletter and everything, and I will not apologize for that. But most of us have swooned over a celebrity or two, and imagined what it would be like to meet them. Well I had a job that not only propelled me into the same stratosphere as the famous, but gave me occasions to actually be equal. I watched so many of today's biggest bands just starting out, hoping to make it themselves.

Eating pizza with a young Rob Thomas from Matchbox 20?

That DID happen!

They weren't Matchbox 20 yet. It was their name, but they weren't yet the household name they'd become. At the time they were just really nice guys who were playing a show for us, and on that day it was my job to make sure they were comfortable and had everything they needed. I was completely clueless this person I was eating pizza with at a picnic table would someday be Rob freakin' Thomas!

These would become my regular, every day work experiences. My best friend Christy was working overnights too, at KROQ in Los Angeles, so she was in the hub of celebrity. Since we had the same schedule we'd talk on the phone most nights. In almost every one of our conversations, Christy would say: "Hold on, someone wants to say Hi," then Jimmy Kimmel would get on the phone, or Moby, or Andy Dick, or the bass player from Green Day—whoever was in her studio at the moment.

Chit chatting with major stars in the middle of the night—this was my new normal!

I would soon learn exactly how few degrees of separation there was between me and "them" when I shared a weird dream I had with my dear friend. I had, very accidentally, dreamt about Bob Saget in an inappropriate way, if you catch my drift. I honestly think it happened because I'd fallen asleep watching America's Funniest Home Videos. (It's the only explanation I can come up with.) Celebrity sex dreams happen to all of us, right? What doesn't usually happen to all of us though, is having the story travel back to the very celebrity who'd rocked your subconscious world. It wasn't long 'til I answered the phone in my studio in Detroit, and heard a voice saying "So exactly how good was I in this dream you had?"

It was Bob Saget on the other end of my phone, and with that I learned to be careful what I told Christy, who seems to know everyone!

I was meeting my favorite rock stars too, and that was surreal. It was people I idolized, people in my wildest dreams I'd never thought I'd meet, let alone connect with. My radio station threw some of the biggest concerts, and every major act at that time was playing shows for us. We had summer concert festivals, and holiday concerts too, every year.

At any of these concerts I could be found playing beer pong with Barenaked Ladies, or helping Sarah McLachlan locate soy milk. "Yeah, I'm just backstage with Sarah talking about kittens, no biggie."

It was one of these shows that provided a bucket list moment for me,—a life altering experience. In a staff meeting at the station, my Program Director was announcing the lineup for our annual holiday show. There were five or six bands on the bill, with a headliner that knocked me off my chair. My boss knew I was obsessed with this band, so I think he was especially excited to tell me.

The Cure would be our headliner!

For me, it didn't get any bigger, and minor hyperventilating took place at the thought of good seats, and maybe a meet and greet, but there would be more! My boss had chosen me to interview Robert Smith. First I threw up in my mouth, and then I begged him to change his mind. It may sound crazy to try to turn down an opportunity like that, but I felt I couldn't be trusted to be that close to the lead singer.

I was supposed to talk to him on the radio? In real time? What a stammering, slobbering, quivering mess this was going to be. This was part of my job. I'd interviewed plenty of rock stars, but this was MY rock star. I was worried for all of us if I was granted this kind of access.

The day arrived, and although I did break out in hives, the minute he walked into the room I instinctively pulled it together. I was sitting in a chair next to his, our knees almost touching, and I was directing this conversation. And he liked me, he really did! I didn't blow it, and the interview went great (I was told) as I could never bring myself to ever go back and listen to it. I stayed professional and I didn't tackle him. It turned out I was pretty good at my job! He even invited me to their after party following the concert. I enthusiastically said "yes," but I was too overstimulated at that point. Any more Robert Smith could've caused a stroke, so I never went.

I've never been big into the backstage, after party, taking pictures part of the business. When I'm required to participate for any or all, obviously I take part, but that's the part of my job that I only need in small doses.

I did have one more personal rock star moment that curled my toes and left a lasting impression on my heart.

I was a huge INXS fan, and had been for many years. I loved their music, and I loved that lead singer. Word came from our PD that INXS was headlining our summer concert, meaning I would be in the vicinity of Michael Hutchence.

Would I be successful a second time at not tackling handsome lead singers?

I was broadcasting live backstage the day of the show and was not expecting to interview any more bands that day. I left to get a drink and when I returned, there were three people standing in this broom closet sized makeshift studio, my boss, one of the members of INXS, and Michael Hutchence.

What was happening?!

My boss looked at me and said, "Are you ready to interview them?"

Was this man trying to kill me? I wasn't even close to ready, but it was my job, so I guessed I'd better get ready. I'd only loved and wanted to marry this man forever, but professionalism somehow happened again, and there would be no stalking charges filed against me that day.

He was so nice to me; there was no rock star attitude whatsoever. I remember him touching my arm, my back my shoulder—you don't forget things like that!

This is where not posing for pictures if I'm not required to bit me in the butt, because I never captured that moment on film. The big hug he gave me, the big beautiful smile he flashed the entire time—I wish I would have gotten that on film, because he died three months to the day of that meeting. I would be one of the last people to interview him, and I feel very fortunate to have that moment, and that memory.

These were my everyday work experiences, and as stunning as they were, I was languishing on overnights. I was so eager to make a name for myself and connect with a larger audience, to have a bigger platform. My boss liked me, and I knew he viewed me as capable, but he remained hesitant to promote me despite the many opportunities. He continued to affirm his intentions to move me to a better time slot, but it never happened, and there were always reasons why.

Finally, I was up for the midday job and I was a natural fit. I lived and breathed the lifestyle, and it seemed a given that I would be promoted to this position. When the job went to someone else, I wasn't the only one who was shocked. I received calls from every radio station in town, from people I had never met, calling to make an introduction and share their own disappointment for me.

DJ's and managers from other radio stations felt strongly enough to call me?

Well maybe I didn't get the promotion, but I made some new friends, and got some much needed validation from around the Detroit dial. I continued to stay patient.

What else could I do?

I sensed that not being a perfect 10 had much to do with my boss's apprehension. It's a tough industry for females who aren't built like swimsuit models. Regardless of how good I was at my job, or how many people I connected with through those radio speakers, there were always going to be managers who factor waist size into the equation.

It's not that I was some underground dwelling creature, I just wasn't a supermodel, and that's, at the very least, a misdemeanor in the entertainment industry.

I was gaining popularity, the audience embraced me, and I became the main fill-in host. I would fill in on the morning show, and all the other day parts, I just couldn't seem to make that leap to permanent host.

Soon, another opportunity came to join the morning show, as the overnight girl didn't work out, which is weird cause she was really hot. And even though I had filled in numerous times, once again I wasn't considered. It was frustrating. I was better for these jobs than the people who would get them. But I'd be given another reason why, and I'd believe it.

Smart woman; clouded judgement.

One more opening became available when I was in the final year of my contract, and this was to host the night show. Doing nights wasn't really where I saw myself, but it was better hours, people were actually listening, and it was a promotion. And that's all I desperately wanted—a promotion. I was the fill-in host while the search was conducted, which was familiar territory. I had been the acting host, the fill-in host, for all the other positions I was vying for.

What's the saying, always the fill-in host never the bride?

Surely my boss was going to give me this job though. He'd been telling me for years that the next opening was, and well you know the rest.

Complicating things slightly was the fact that Darren was also being considered, and he'd been waiting for a long time to be promoted, too. So here I was in contention for the same position as my friend.

As I continued doing nights, I really didn't like it. It wasn't what I was supposed to be doing, and I decided that I'd be fine if Darren got the job. A decision came three months later and I received a call one evening at home. It was my boss.

"What are you doing right now?" he asked.

"Cutting vegetables," I replied.

"So you have a knife in your hand huh?" he continued, and we both laughed.

He was calling to tell me that Darren was getting the job, but that it came down to a coin toss. Darren wasn't full time and didn't have benefits, and this would be an opportunity to make that happen for him. I was disappointed all the other times I missed out on the job, but not this time, and I told my boss that. I really was happy for Darren, and the bonus was that I'd get to see him every day.

So once again, I became the overnight mistress of darkness, banished back to my original shift. When I saw Darren I gave him a big hug and genuinely enthusiastic congratulations. I was really happy for him. He deserved good things. But Darren had had a change of heart, and decided he did not want the job after all. I asked him if he was sure it was what he wanted, and it was. He was positive that he was making the right choice for himself. He was calling our boss the next day, before any contracts were signed, and would be declining the offer.

At that point he started to congratulate me, it came down to a coin toss, so clearly I would be getting a call the next day, too. I would be moving to more "respectable" hours, a better time slot, and a raise!

When you do overnights, the graveyard shift, you don't go to bed until six or seven in the morning, so you don't wake up until late afternoon. It was after three when I woke up the next day, excited to run and check my answering machine, but it wasn't flashing.

Darren must have called our boss by now, where was my call?

Maybe it was busy around the office, maybe there will be a message for me when I get to work, and this would all make sense soon. There wasn't a message at work, or a phone call the next day, or the day after that, or ever. I didn't need this spelled out for me. It wasn't a hard puzzle to put together. I wasn't getting this job, and I had never really been considered. I found out several people had been asked to take the job after Darren rejected it, and they all turned it down, too. It finally went to someone who had been fired all those years ago on "Black Monday".

That news was great; he was a good friend of mine who never should have been fired in the first place. What wasn't great was the realization that I was never going to move from overnights as long as I worked for this program director. I'm sure he liked me enough, and he'd kept me so that was something, but he was never going to see me as more than the middle of the night girl. And I was so much more than that.

I was really good at my job, and this was exactly what I was meant to be doing, on a much larger platform. That was my destiny, but it wasn't going to happen under the current PD. So it became clear to me, right then and there that I was going to have to leave. If I was going to make it, I'd have to walk away from this radio station. I decided that on the day my contract was up that's just what I'd do. There would be no conversations about resigning, just a "thanks for everything," and this part of the story would be over. I didn't have any plans for what I'd do next; I didn't know where I would go. I was kind of hoping the universe would intervene again, that fate would step in as it had all those times before.

That probably doesn't seem like the most practical way to plan your life, but hey, if it ain't broke, don't fix it. Someone upstairs was moving us around like chess pieces, because fate really was about to smile on me again. Most would probably just call it a fortunate coincidence, but either way, good things were about to happen.

We were all gathered into the conference room again, where departures and arrivals had been announced before for another shocking revelation.

My program director was leaving!

He'd taken another job across the country and in a week or so he'd be gone. And just like that, four months shy of my own plan to exit, he was saying goodbye. I remember riding down in the elevator with him on his last day and it feeling slightly awkward, but I had no hard feelings, as I knew my "meant to be" was coming. Sometimes you're just not someone's cup of tea, and I wasn't his. But I was about to be someone's, in a really big way.

Enter, Tom.

Chapter Ten

WHO WAS THAT MASKED MAN?

It seems almost crazy that I was preparing to walk away from such a good job, a dream job really. A job working at this radio station, in this market, for this company, where on any given day I could be interacting with random celebrities. But that wasn't enough for me, I didn't want to bask in other people's success, I wanted my own. I was having amazing experiences, but these experiences weren't furthering my career, and I needed to start making moves for my own future.

If I did walk away, what guarantee was there that I would ever be hired again?

It's not like these types of jobs are so easy to come by. They are in very high demand, with hundreds of people all vying for any and all openings. It would definitely be risky to walk away from a second radio station in pursuit of my dreams, but sometimes you have to take a leap of faith, and believe in yourself enough to walk away from something not worthy of you.

Whitney Houston was right, the greatest love of all is inside of me, and even if no one saw my full potential, I did, and I wasn't going to settle for less.

Fortunately, instead of having to roll the dice and leave in search of greener pastures, now I was preparing to meet with the new guy. He was my fourth program director, and I was meeting with him in the same office the previous two had occupied, the office where my journey at this radio station began.

How does that saying go? People may forget the things you said, but they will never forget how you made them feel? I think Maya Angelou said it, and how true it is.

I'll never forget how Tom made me feel from the moment we met. I got off the elevator on the 21st floor and made my way to the office for our introduction. I turned the corner and was almost knocked over by his presence. He was standing in the middle of the program area, and he was one of the tallest people I'd ever met who wasn't a pro athlete. He had the most sincere, wide smile, and he just beamed good energy and light, like an Aurora Borealis. We locked eyes, and even though we hadn't yet met he knew who I was, and this towering figure made his way toward me with open arms. We proceeded to hug it out like family members at a holiday reunion. Tom was a hugger, and so was I, so this was a match made in heaven.

I'll never forget the very first words my new boss said to me on that first day we met:

"Why are you doing overnights?"

Tom knew me, he knew all of us, as he hadn't traveled far to take this program director job. He held the same position across the street working for one of our competitors. Tom had been in Detroit for a very long time, observing our station and forming opinions long before the opportunity to work there ever became available, and one of his opinions was that it made no sense for me to be doing overnights.

For 6 years I couldn't make a move, and now in the blink of an eye everything was about to change with the arrival of Tom. There was a new program director, a new vision, a new direction for the radio station, and I was going to take center stage.

There wasn't going to be another "Black Monday," but Tom was definitely going to make some staff changes. He would also change the music and the format of the radio station. Tom was brilliant, I'm sure he still is, and he was one of the smartest programmers I've ever worked for. I just trusted that he was putting us on the path to success.

For as cool of a radio station as we were, our ratings never impressed. We were doing big things, and got a lot of attention, but alternative radio stations don't captivate the larger audience. It's a niche format which tends to attract a smaller and specific audience. Tom started tweaking our music to what is called a Hot AC format. He also changed our call letters and the overall identity of the radio station.

Around this time we also moved several floors down within the building, after the company had completed building beautiful new studios on the 7th and 8th floors. The view wasn't as good as it was when we were at the very top, but these were state of the art studios unlike anything we'd ever seen before. This was ABC/Disney quality stuff. Essentially, I was now working at a brand new radio station without ever having to leave the building!

That's a pretty cool party trick right? If I could bottle and sell that I'd make a fortune!

Staff changes were about to take place too, and many of the personalities my last boss brought on board weren't going to make the cut, starting with the morning show. I knew I fit into Toms plans, he'd as much as told me so, but I never would have guessed how quickly and how prominently.

My phone rang one afternoon and it was Tom. He had fired the morning show earlier that day and was calling with a new work assignment for me, starting the very next day. I would be doing mornings. Talk about showing faith in my abilities!

I wasn't going to be the permanent morning show host, as he had plans to assemble a new team, but until that was complete I would be the holding down the fort. I just went from overnights to mornings in seconds flat! I'm sorry can you repeat that? Starting tomorrow I host the morning show in the sixth largest market in the country?

Actually I think Detroit had fallen to seventh place by then, but these are minor details. Doing mornings in a top ten market? By myself? *Tomorrow?*

It proves one thing, we should always be prepared for amazing opportunities, because they can show up when we least expect them—maybe when we're just about to give up altogether.

I was going to make the most of the opportunity that was for sure.

I had waited so many years for any kind of forward movement, and now I'd just made the biggest move of all, and for as long as it took my boss to develop a new show, I was going to be the voice of mornings. Detroit and I were about to get much more acquainted and I was ready to knock some socks off!

The recently fired morning show had developed a following over the five years they were on the air, so their fans were obviously upset over their dismissal, and they were making their feelings known. I was a couple of months into hosting mornings when the programming assistant started bringing me stacks of emails to read—angry emails from their fans. It probably seems odd that she'd want me to see those emails, especially since I had sort of replaced them, but every single disgruntled email ended the same way, "...but Allyson is doing a great job, we don't blame her." Literally every single email (and there were many) ended with some sort of compliment for me! And that meant a lot! It reaffirmed that I really was doing a good job, because these people were pissed that their favorite show was gone. I was getting positive feedback from the audience, and I was also getting it, in an odd way, from upper management too.

I have a vivid memory of our general manager walking past the studio and giddily exclaiming "I'm never getting a morning show!" That backhanded compliment came after the ratings showed that my little "overnight show in the morning" experiment was resonating with the listeners. I never did find out exactly how well I was doing in the ratings, but our GM didn't get giddy very often.

There was a dark cloud hanging over all of this personal good fortune though, because what fun would it be if everything went exactly the way you wanted it to right?

The radio station was in the process of making many changes, including attempting to hire a major morning personality currently in the market. I knew this wasn't what Tom wanted but he had bosses too, and if this morning host accepted the offer it would mean a format flip, and we would all be out of a job. We were all on pins and needles awaiting the outcome.

While I was having this career high, with the promise of a bright future now that Tom was here, it all rested on whether or not this popular morning host would make my station his new radio home.

We weren't the only station trying to lure him, as other stations also wanted to hire this well-known personality, but this was ABC/ Disney in The Fisher Building, of course he was going to want to work there.

It was quiet around the station at this time. Management was doing their best to avoid interaction with the staff, knowing this deal would put us all out on the street. This ominous mood was really killing my morning show buzz, but I had to keep the faith. Faith had been a part of my journey from the very beginning, so I had to believe I couldn't have come this far to have it all snatched away now.

We waited for what felt like an eternity when the good news was finally delivered! The morning host had taken another offer and would not be coming here. We avoided a total flip and a trip to the unemployment line.

Grandma was that you again?

I had been doing mornings for about nine months, and my contract had long expired, but I remained patient. I would be taken care of when the dust settled, I just knew it.

Soon, it was time to finally unveil the new morning show. Our company was moving a show out of New York to Detroit to fill the vacancy, and nine months after the last show exited, a new one came aboard. Tom had had different plans for mornings, though.

He had wanted to create an all-female morning show that resembled the TV show "The View". Tom was a visionary, and an out of the box thinker, and he wasn't afraid to try things that no one else was doing. And this definitely would have been a new concept for a morning show, but the company made a different call, and the New York show moved to Detroit.

I don't know if I would have had a place on the all-female morning show, since we never got that far, but it was time to find a place for me now that the new morning show was ready to go. I couldn't go back to overnights, could I? I'd successfully hosted the morning show for close to a year, so clearly I'd proven myself, and Tom believed in me, but currently there wasn't anything else available.

One afternoon, I got another phone call at home from Tom. He had really good news. I was really starting to like these calls at home from Tom! I think he was just as excited to deliver the news as I was to hear it, as it had been a long time coming—a very long time. My talking on the radio while everybody else slept officially ended that day. Tom was calling to tell me that I was the brand new midday host beginning the next day!

At this point there was a lot of shrieking on my end of the phone, causing a lot of cats to scatter!

It was another one of those bittersweet moments though, as my promotion meant someone else was losing their job. And the next day Tom had to tell the current host that it was his last day, at the very moment my role as his replacement began.

Radio is tough, these are the hard parts.

The job I'd been passed over on for years before was now mine, and soon I was signing my second five year contract. Another five years!

We were morphing into this brand new station, and I was signing on for five more years. Life can change real fast.

It almost feels like Tom had come there just to help me, because it wasn't long after the ink dried on my contract that he was gone. Right as I was about to walk away from that place, he showed up out of nowhere, and the minute I was safely secured in my new position he was gone. Just like that.

At the time he was building this radio station into a force to be reckoned with, he was also dealing with personal issues, and addressing them was his number one priority. Soon I'd be reading an email from corporate that Tom was no longer employed by the company. I was heartbroken, not just for me, but for all of us. I didn't even get to say goodbye.

There's no doubt he would have made the radio station #1, we were just lucky enough to have him get us on the right path. I probably wasn't going to ever have another boss who'd walk by my studio, push the door wide open, and say, smiling brightly, "How's my girl today?"

But I'm so glad that, for a little while, I did.

Chapter Eleven

SOUL PATROL

It was kind of a revolving door for the next few years: interim program directors, new program directors, new general managers, constant changes. Normally you have to keep changing jobs to have so many different bosses, or coworkers that changed so frequently, but I just stayed in one place while things continued to change around me. There was always stress when new management took the reigns as they could change everything with the snap of their fingers, which I'd certainly seen so many times before. Even though I was already employed, my job hung in the balance with every new boss that came through.

I had a few things working in my favor though, giving me a little security. I had signed a new contract, so that was a bit of security. I was also experiencing a personal career high!

My midday show was #1 in Detroit, and I consistently ranked in the top spot in the ratings!

Being able to prove that when given the chance, I would always succeed was empowering. I was given all of the big assignments as the morning show from New York wasn't doing well at all. They weren't connecting with the Detroit audience, and in turn began isolating themselves from the rest of the station. It was just going to be a matter of time before yet another morning show would be gone. The producer of the show was a nice guy. He tried to maintain relationships with the rest of us. He would often come into my studio after their show was over and he'd say, "Sorry about what we did to your ratings."

Although I sympathized with his struggles, it kind of made me feel good. It validated that my nine month morning show run was not only successful but word of my ratings had gotten around. I was doing things that morning shows would normally do, and I was having the time of my life! I was broadcasting live aboard Disney cruise ships on 4 and 7 day cruises, and also broadcasting annually from Disney World, too. I was going on the press junkets for TV shows and movie premiers, and interviewing the stars, and I was even handling the live broadcasts from the Big House for the Michigan home games. Broadcasting live from football games didn't seem like something I'd be picked for, but I rocked it!

I was going to make sure whatever assignment I was given, I would give 100% and make sure it was flawless. It seemed I always had to work harder than everyone else, so I just got used to that, whether it was fair or not. I was never going to give anyone the chance to see even the most minor crack. I soon developed a close relationship with our new general manager, and he was another person I could add to the list of bosses who saw my full potential.

I even played manager for a period of time after my GM fired the latest program director. Until a replacement was found, I was holding down the fort, and became responsible for scheduling. If you called in sick or needed time off, you called me, and each week I'd have the schedule done and posted so everyone knew when they were working. It was a big responsibility. I'm not even sure how I figured out how to do it, but somehow I did, and for a short time I was a fair and benevolent manager.

Lots of changes were on the horizon again, and I did my best to stay calm. After all, look how much I'd done for that station! I used to have this silly belief that all of your good and hard work was being noticed by all of those above you. (Silly girl.) But I'd survived this far, and I was going the distance.

The morning show was eventually fired, and a new one was put in its place. We would get a new program director, and there were rumblings that the company was selling us.

NO! Working for ABC/Disney was amazing, they couldn't sell us! I prayed, "Come on Michael Eisner, don't let this happen, I'm really digging these yearly cruises and trips to Disney World."

Before that could happen, I found myself in what was now a familiar position— meeting my new boss. I wasn't exactly sure what number we were on at that point, I think he was my 6th or 7th program director. Ron had come from across the country and I remember feeling uneasy about that at first. The last guy from out of town with no Detroit ties never promoted me, so I was hoping against all hope that I wasn't going to experience a backslide. (Ron was also really tall, and that was a good sign—the last really tall guy loved me!)

How Ron felt about me landed somewhere in the middle. I think in the early days he tolerated me. But Ron and I had many years in front of us, and we were going to eventually make radio magic together. Despite the fact that my midday show was consistently #1, and by now I had developed a pretty loyal fan base, I was once again not my new boss's cup of tea.

I think he just had a specific style that he liked, and I may or may not have possessed that style, at least for that position. And in the early days I may have been a minor pain in his ass by constantly forgetting it was EVERY Tuesday he wanted to meet in his office for an air check session.

Air checks are mini progress reports. We listen to a tape of my show together and my PD points out what he likes about my show, or what he doesn't like, or what he really doesn't like. I thought, "Being #1 is good enough, must we go through these silly exercises?" Thankfully Ron was an extremely patient man, which was one of his many wonderful qualities.

Shortly after Ron's arrival, I reached a personal career milestone at the radio station, celebrating my ten year anniversary. I had ten years in one place, with constant change around me, and so much upheaval. Still, I remained in place.

How had so much time passed so quickly?

And in those ten years I had fought so hard just to get where I was, a mere stepping stone to where I was meant to be. Would Ron be impressed by this milestone? Would it make him want to keep me on as part of his team? Well he was the one to deliver my plaque, so I think he recognized my accomplishment. Disney actually honored this milestone with a gorgeous plaque commemorating my decade with the station/ company, and in a staff meeting in front of everyone Ron presented it to me. It was a nice moment, and of course I keep that with the special Mickey Mouse pen. I'm sappy sentimental that way.

Disney also presented me with a ten year pin. Boy, was I going to miss that company. And it wouldn't be long until it finally happened, and they did in fact sell us. My plaque and pin would be my last Disney perks. It was a great experience working for a company that showed gratitude to long time employees that way.

This kind of recognition would go the way of the dodo bird in radio's future. We were property of a new radio company now, and we were very lucky to have as part of the terms of the sale, an agreement that nothing be changed for the next two years. It was an added insurance policy for the workers of the company that we wouldn't be blown out the minute the new owners took over. We could all breathe easy for at least the next two years, a nice parting gift from the company that had always treated us so well.

We had two years to make this radio station a powerhouse, one that the new owners wouldn't want to change even once they could. And that meant there was work to do.

Ron didn't just have a sassy midday girl to reign in, he also had a struggling morning show to deal with. Yes, once again we had a morning show that was not connecting with the Detroit audience. It was starting to feel like this station had been cursed by the morning show gods. It had been close to two years since this new show replaced the New York show, yet ratings showed no improvement, and consistently ranked in the very bottom of the ratings. The morning show didn't have much time left and Ron was going to try to save it if he could. No one likes to have to fire people, (well unless you're that guy from the beginning of this book).

Around this time there was a contestant on the current season of American Idol whom I didn't like very much. She'd made it to the top 4 or 5 and I remember being bothered by that. This was in the heyday of American Idol, when it dominated conversation, and this season was particularly controversial. On occasion I would join the morning show for their last break, right before they'd turn things over to me, and I'd go on a little American Idol rant. It was just silly fun, venting about one of the most popular TV shows at the time, and my incredibly strong feelings about one of the contestants. Doing this once or twice led to me being asked for more interaction on the show. I was even asked to wake up early, before my alarm would go off, so I could call into the show.

I'm one of sleeps biggest fans! I do not like to part with any slumber I have coming to me, so getting up before my scheduled time made me a little itchy, but I was happy to help. If Ron thought my AI recaps were helpful then I would absolutely accommodate. American Idol came to an end just a few weeks later, so I no longer had a reason to vent. I was the one person in America who believed the right person won that season and I won't apologize for that either.

There was no reason for me to join in on the morning show now that there was no AI to discuss, but Ron decided that my presence had made a difference, and he wanted to continue down this path. He came into my studio one morning and asked me how I felt about moving to the morning show on a trial basis, so he could get an idea of what "more Allyson" would sound like.

I don't want to toot my own horn, but my last two morning shows were pretty successful. I think it's fair to say you can never go wrong with more Allyson. ;)

I wanted not only to prove myself to Ron, but I knew that I could absolutely make a difference. I'd done it before. And when I accomplished that goal the sky was going to be the limit for me!

Mornings and beyond was always my "meant to be."

There was also a great risk in taking this assignment as this morning show didn't have much time left. Replacing them was already being discussed by management, and if this experiment did not work, I had no guarantee that I would get my midday position back. As a matter of fact it was more likely that I wouldn't. I've never been afraid of a challenge, I was always ready to prove myself, and I knew this was another nudge from the universe.

This was no accident, this was destiny. Hello old friend!

Who knew having such unusually strong feelings about a singing competition show could play such a pivotal role in my future? I finished my last midday show that day, knowing I was never coming back to this position.

Would it be because I succeeded, or would it be because time ran out?

I was about to roll the dice and find out.

Chapter Twelve

PREPARE FOR LIFTOFF AND A KICK IN THE TEETH

I was off like a rocket the minute I sat in the morning show chair. After all, it was not my first time at this rodeo. Mornings had been my destiny from the very beginning of this journey. I'd had my own show twice before and always received positive response from the audience. I had been there for a long time, twelve years at that point. I cared about each and every one of our listeners, and they cared about me in return.

The needle moved instantly, on the first day I joined the show, and there was no looking back.

This show was destined for greatness. It was an exciting time, knowing that we were on the right track, though not everyone was happy with this new arrangement. Some would rather have been fired than to watch me be welcomed by the audience with such open arms. But that's the nature of this business—jealousy, insecurity, not playing well with others in the sandbox; it's an unfortunate byproduct. The more popular I became publicly, the more my character took a hit behind the scenes, and soon colorful tales of how awful I was (the other side of Allyson) were being told on a daily basis by spiteful coworkers, to anyone who would listen.

Now that I'd finally arrived where I belonged, of course there would be a sinister coworker to deal with. Why should I expect smooth sailing?

At first it was amusing. Who would believe this nonsense? I'm as open a book as can be. There is no other side, I put it all out there—

warts and all. What should have been a happy adventure, putting this morning show on the map, now was covered with a dark cloud. It was a difficult time for me.

Normally, when someone is trying to destroy me, I don't take too kindly to that. Wasn't it one of the Real Housewives that said, "Don't come for me unless I send for you"—? So now I'm quoting real housewives, but you get the point. I don't usually sit idly by while others attempt to assassinate my character, or cause harm to my career.

I've worked really hard for people to know who I am, and what I stand for, and I've earned my good reputation.

This wasn't fair to me, especially since in closed quarters it was always smiles and sunshine, and "I'm so glad you're here." I was proud of myself though, and of how uncharacteristically well I was handling this situation. This morning show wasn't given a lot of time to produce results. We didn't have a moment to waste on petty bickering over other people's jealousy, and the nonsense that was taking place.

I don't always travel "the high road" with such ease—getting petty is one of my strong suits. I don't like to brag, but I can get petty with the best of them. I somehow found the strength to rise above it and stayed focused on the mission. I could only hope that people would reject the smear campaign being launched my way. For as hard as it was to hear such vile things about myself, or watch people I considered friends buy into it hook, line and sinker, I had a job to do. I'd waited a long time to get back in this chair, so "Go ahead and hate me because I'm good at my job, I'm going to focus on the task at hand; winning!"

The entire experience did reaffirm one of my own philosophies though, which is "the high road is for suckers". I should have been putting an end to that BS every step of the way! The whole "kill em' with kindness" strategy? Well I tried it, and it just gave them a head start.

So I was back to "the high road is for suckers". I made that one up. Do you like it? I'm thinking of putting it on bumper stickers.

The morning show was on the verge of blowing up in the very best way, but we had come really close to coming off the rails for good. Fortunately the universe wasn't going to let that happen. Thanks to the kindness of strangers, whom much like Blanch Dubois I'd also always depended on, this mini nightmare was about to come to an end.

One evening at home, actually quite late, my phone rang, and it was one of the most surreal calls I'd ever received. On the other end of the phone was one of Detroit's top news anchors. He was very well known, very well respected, and someone I'd never met before. Obviously, I knew this person the same way everyone else did, from watching them on TV. It's not completely out of the ordinary for people in our business to reach out to each other, as we were colleagues in a way, but it was after hours, and how did this person get my phone number anyway?

This was my "A-ha" moment. This was when it became clear that I couldn't sit by and allow my reputation to be damaged any further. The news anchor was a fan of mine, had been following my career for years, and gave me praise and credit for the morning show becoming the success it had become. They'd heard the stories of what a "workplace monster" I was, and knew it didn't jive with the person they'd listened to all this time. They knew that there couldn't be a kernel of truth to it. And this was the reason for the call. They felt strongly that all the back talk was an attempt to make a case against me, to harm me professionally, to have me removed.

Friendly advice was given.This was from someone who'd been in the business for decades, and had seen this happen before. I was told to document all incidents, and keep my HR person in the loop, and above all, "Don't let it crush your gentle spirit." That is an exact quote, and it validated that who I really was came through the speakers, and couldn't be manipulated through twisted tales.

People knew the truth.

I just remember being in awe that someone of that stature would go out of their way to help me, and to look out for me. This was someone

I'd never met, and never really had much interaction with following that conversation, but I was left dumbfounded by their actions. There are good people in the world who put their necks on the line even for strangers.

I had faith again.

I also had newly acquired strength to stop the BS immediately. We were just about to go on Christmas break, and we and gathered in Ron's office for a final, end of the year meeting. With everyone present, I made it clear that when we came back from vacation, a choice would have to be made. I would no longer continue to work my ass of for this place all the while being vilified unfairly.

"So take this time to decide who you want, because this ends here, today."

You could have heard a pin drop after that, it was just silence. Ron expected to have a, "It's been a great year, next year's going to be even better," kind of meeting, and instead I was sending us into the holiday with bombshells and ultimatums. It had been a long time coming, and if no one else was going to put an end to it, me and my new anchor friend would.

"Merry Christmas, everyone."

Extreme kindness was shown to me in that phone call by someone who didn't know me, but still cared. That's the kind of person I'd always tried to be, and when I was in need, kindness came back to me. Looking out for each other is a powerful thing. It's so much better than tearing each other down.

We went on vacation as scheduled, and in the New Year everything kind of seamlessly worked out. People went this way, people went that way, and peace was finally restored. I'd like to say it would be the last time I'd have to deal with that kind of treatment, but it wouldn't be. Taylor swift sings "People throw rocks at things that shine", and it's an unfortunate truth.

I hadn't see the last of the rock throwers, and I certainly wasn't going to stop shining.

Chapter Thirteen

A GIRL AND A CITY

Detroit is a powerful market filled with legendary broadcasters and popular shows. It was an intimidating task not only to compete in this market but to win, and it was a task I was taking very seriously. I felt such a connection to this city, not just because of the 12 years I'd already spent here, but because Detroit was making a comeback. This was a city on the rise, the little engine that could!

Do not ever count Detroit out!

And I had that same spirit myself. I'd spent most of my time at this radio station fighting to get back to mornings, to prove it was where I belonged, and I wasn't giving up either. Detroit would prove everyone wrong, and I was about to do the same.

It's the Motor City, people love their cars, and commutes can be anywhere from 15 minutes to 2 ½ hours. We spend a lot of time in our cars and we form serious relationships with our radio personalities and the shows that we listen to. Strong bonds are formed. Maybe this happens in other markets, but it is very prevalent in Detroit.

I had already formed a bond with my listeners over the years, but I was meeting all kinds of new people now, and I wanted to make our relationship monogamous.

"I'm feeling pretty serious about you Detroit, let's take things to the next level."

The audience had great shows to choose from already, how was I going to stand out? The dial was filled with some of the best radio has to offer, a mustachioed radio legend whose name is synonymous with broadcasting, a dynamic duo, kings of radio who'd been ruling the airwaves for decades, and a bestselling author responsible for writing one of Oprah's favorite books.

These shows were examples of the significant radio landscape occupying Detroit. So what could I possibly bring to the table to win over the audience? Whatever the strategy was going to be, it was going to be a cheap strategy. This show was not going to have a budget, really no monetary assistance at all. There would be no marketing for the show or even any stand out promotions. The radio station had gone through one sale already, and we were about to be sold again. So this show, that not so long ago sat at the very bottom of the ratings pile was going to have to find a winning formula that required zero backing.

That was going to definitely be a challenge, but I hadn't backed down from a challenge yet. There would be no billboards, and no TV commercials. This was going to be a grass roots movement. And it was, as everything really did begin very organically, with simple basic principles:

- Genuinely care about who you are talking to and they will genuinely care back.

- Get involved with the community, be a part of helping rebuild this great city, and share your whole self with the audience.

- No putting on airs, give the real, everyday details of the life you live, don't be afraid to share your strong opinions, stand up for things that matter, and be respectful to those who think differently.

- Oh and be funny if you can. People like to laugh in the morning. People NEED to laugh in the morning.

- The audience is working hard, holding down numerous jobs, raising families, trying to do it all, and in the winter dealing with some pretty brutal temperatures. Yeah, they need to laugh.

- The audience wants to know that you are going through the same things that they are going through.

- Be mindful of little ears in the car—it really is possible to be edgy in a way that goes right over those little heads.

- And read the emails you get from your listeners. More importantly answer their emails.

- — and if you can do a dead on Kim Kardashian impression don't be afraid to use it. But use it in small doses, obviously.

Almost everything about this morning show involved everyday life, as if we were sitting at my kitchen table, having coffee and talking. This format was resonating with the listeners. This type of show wasn't really being done in the morning, so I had found my niche!

More and more people were tuning in, and even better, they were coming back the following day. And the one thing I had worked for, for such a long time, finally happened—my morning show became #1! From the bottom of the barrel to the very top of the heap, this morning show had hit the top spot in the ratings, and for many years after would stay there.

Ron took a gamble on me, that I could turn things around in the morning, and here we were celebrating a number one morning show. This radio station hadn't had a number one morning show in a very long time, and I felt proud to be able to show those who believed in me, (and even those who didn't) that I could do that. The show had a huge fan base, as did the radio station overall, and Ron was turning the place into a powerhouse. We were firing on all cylinders! Our midday show was the best, out afternoon show was the best, our night show was—well you get the picture. All of our on air personalities were crushing it, earning top ratings themselves.

I had been in love with this radio station long before I sent that lone cassette tape in an attempt to be hired. I had always wanted to see it win, to see it respected and admired, and that was really happening.

We even started to see copycat stations/shows. That is the most sincere form of flattery, right? I think I found it more annoying than flattering, but it proved we were worth duplicating. Everyone had worked hard to turn out one hell of a product, and it couldn't have come at a better time.

You see, once again, we were sold to another radio company, and we all knew what that could potentially mean. So here we go again, behind the scenes frustration and panic set in over the sale of our station, now to a third company.

And when this sale was complete there will be no insurance policy like the one Disney worked out with the last company. Everyone's future was up in the air, so it was a very good time to be #1.

It seemed no matter how much success I was achieving I still couldn't get "there", to that place where I could enjoy it, bask in it. I wasn't receiving the respect that someone who'd turned a morning show around deserved, and I certainly wasn't being paid what a top morning host should be paid. I was consistently beating other shows that made bank—six figures into millions.

I'm embarrassed to even hint at what I was making. Remember that lesson I learned early on when my radio journey first began? Being a woman in this business was going to be a detriment, because what could a woman do anyway? I don't know, she could be the first radio personality in at least two decades to take this morning show to number one. She could develop a winning strategy that caused a city, a neighboring country, and throngs of fans across the country to flock to a radio station.

I'd say a woman could do a whole hell of a lot.

I've never been a good self-promoter. I've always waited for someone else to give me credit, to acknowledge my contributions, but that hadn't happened, and it wasn't going to. So, here I am shouting self-praise from the rooftop.

I did a remarkable thing by my little old self—good job Allyson!

And for my ladies out there who don't get the credit they deserve for doing it all—working that job, raising that family, being the glue that keeps it all together—there is no one else like you! You make the world go round!

Yes we did just have a Beyoncé moment!

I kept thinking I'd just keep working hard, deliver a winning product and right around the corner would be the Valhalla that I worked for. Well, there certainly would be more around the corner.

I don't think I'd describe it as Valhalla, though.

Whatever else was going on, there was one thing that couldn't be denied which gave me great pride, and for which I was so grateful. I had developed a really powerful relationship with my listeners. I'd find out down the road just how powerful. And if I couldn't get the proper credit or "equal to my peers" paychecks, at least I had the audience—my audience.

The brand new company was coming soon and there I was, sitting there, still being a woman. Well, I could always do some light housework or laundry when my show was done, right?

The new company taking over wasn't the only thing on the horizon as something else was about to happen to my radio show.

Across the country, in the land of sun and celebrity, a producer was creating a TV show, and ears in Hollywood had been listening to my show for quite a while. L.A. was about to meet Detroit.

Make sure to have a Coney and a Faygo while you're in town.

Chapter Fourteen

LIGHTS, CAMERA, ACTION

When I was just 4 or 5 years old, my mom predicted I would have my own TV talk show when I grew up. She also believed her oh-so-smart-and-special child could be a lawyer someday, too. What did she see in little Allyson to fill her with such pride and give her such hope for my future? It turns out these are just perfect jobs for people who love to talk and argue, and she likes to say I came into the delivery room doing both.

And though I did represent Barbie in numerous cases against random stuffed animals with the judge always ruling in our favor, it was always the "talk" road I was traveling.

My radio show was the epitome of success, with no signs of slowing down. Behind the scenes the battle for respect, fair pay, and troublesome coworkers raged on, but at this particular time in my career we'd come as close to "the good years" as we were going to get. I felt such pride to deliver a product that not only was warmly embraced by the audience, but one that now, other shows were trying to duplicate. Under Ron's leadership we felt like a family, a real team, playing in the World Series, and we had each other's backs.

So when the general manager wanted a meeting in his office there was no reason to panic. Normally you don't want to get emails that your GM wants to see you, but we were a tight group, and this was a radio station on fire, so this meeting could only be positive. Positive was an understatement! This meeting was going to change my life forever.

It had been awhile since the hands of fate had shaken up my

world, but it seemed as if the universe was about to smile on me once again. What was about to happen, again, was one of those things that just don't happen, especially here.

We assembled in my GM's office where he proceeded to tell us about a television producer who'd recently contacted him regarding a show he was developing. The concept was a half hour comedy/ entertainment show featuring top morning shows across the country discussing the celebrity gossip of the day. The producer had done months and months of research, listening to morning shows across the country in an effort to find the right shows for his project. And I'll be damned if Detroit wasn't about to get another win in our column! The producer loved my show and was sending a film crew to Detroit to film a pilot.

Detroit would be featured on an entertainment show? People make jokes about Detroit, they don't include Detroit on nationally syndicated television shows. Or maybe they do, and I was being picked to be a part of this show. It was only a concept at that moment, but if it all worked out, on a nightly basis, the rest of the country could see just how great the D was. I was so ready for this challenge. It was the blink of an eye between the meeting in my GM's office and filming the pilot. It happened that quickly.

Before we knew it L.A. was rolling into the Fisher Building with their cameras and their boom mics and their key grips, (if that is a real thing). I'm sure many shows were tapped to film pilots. I wasn't fooling myself into thinking it was just us, but I was determined to make them fall in love with Detroit. I even got all gussied up, from head to toe, down to the fake nails I glued on myself.

I couldn't make the full manicure commitment just yet. Until I found out if being a TV star was in my future, the six dollar box of nails would have to do for now. And then we filmed the pilot.

And then we waited.

Was it good enough? Was I funny enough? Would Hollywood

like us? It was all I could think about until we heard back, and when we finally heard back the answer was yes, yes, and yes! Detroit would be featured in the six week test run of a new celebrity gossip style show. There would be four morning shows from across the country that would be featured; 3 of your major cities with Detroit rounding out the cast.

This is what over the moon feels like, huh?

The radio audience went on this journey with us, and we shared every single step with them on the radio show. After all, it was their journey, too. My feeling was that I'd been picked to represent my city, and I wanted to make sure that I made the listeners proud. The six week test run would air during the summer in select markets, and if it was well received then we'd become a real TV show.

We'd be a real TV show airing weeknights in living rooms across the country, not select markets, but everywhere!

So at 11:30 p.m. you could watch Seinfeld reruns, the Tonight show, or me? I felt like I was going to need a team of people to pinch me. This was as surreal as it gets.

Before long L.A. arrived back in Detroit, and for the next six weeks we made a really funny TV show. While we did the morning show, cameras would film us for the TV show, then later that evening what we'd done that morning was on the small screen.

I came in early every day for hair and makeup, (a far cry from the pajama type clothes and hair in a bun that I usually sported for work). My makeup artist was amazing, and she was a big deal in her own right. She worked on major motion pictures, and did the makeup for the biggest movie stars. And the magic she could work on my jacked up eyebrows was astounding! I was in the makeup chair for an hour and a half every morning before our 5:30 a.m. start time. I have a new appreciation for models—it really is work getting your makeup done all the time. I never thought I'd say that.

Our field producer, Jason, would then go over the stories we were to do that day. We'd try to do as many stories as we could live on the radio show, and the rest we would perform for the cameras while in music or commercial breaks. Those were called "pick-ups" (that's Hollywood lingo). We made great TV, and laughed every day. Even back at the hub in LA they were laughing with us! Word was that Detroit was the favorite of the editors and producers that put the show together. Kevin and Ed, our cameramen, and Jason our field producer were soon like family. It's amazing how close you can become with new people in six short weeks. This TV crew had become part of my radio show too, especially Jason.

On the final day of filming, with the test run now over, there were lots of tears as we were saying goodbye. We knew we'd done a great job, and everyone was happy with our work—most of all the creator of the show. There was just nothing but love after the six weeks. But this wasn't in our hands anymore, the control was now in the hands of the studios.

Would they want this show? Would they back it? Would they put it on TV permanently?

It was too much to believe it could really happen, and if it didn't, I'd already had the experience of my life. I'd filmed a pilot. I'd filmed a six week test run, and I was on TV every night all summer long. I'd already had so many blessings, I was afraid to be greedy and ask for more —not to mention I still had my number one rated morning show!

Yeah, this probably wasn't going to happen, one girl cannot have that much luck. I stayed casual about the whole thing. if it happened great, if not, well that's great, too. We all stayed in contact with each other, our little TV family, as this show getting picked up meant jobs for everyone. Jason would come back, Kevin and Ed would come back, and J, my magical makeup artist would come back. We'd all be together again. We would periodically check with each other to see if anyone had heard anything, and we'd wait, and we'd wait, and we'd—well you get it.

My listeners were so great too! They sent so much energy and so many prayers out to us, hopeful this dream would really happen. They had supported the TV show for the duration of the test run, and they continued to be hopeful. Detroit was behind this show, and I knew the audience had everything to do with what happened next.

The TV show featuring four radio morning shows from across the country dishing celebrity gossip had been picked up!

What I'd like to do now is fill the rest of this page with exclamation points and smiley faces but I remind myself this is a book, not a personal email, so I won't.

We finally got word in January from the creator of the show. This project was his baby, and he informed us that the hard work we'd poured into this—the love, the devotion, the funny—it paid off! We were going to be on a full time TV show, it was picked up, and we could add "TV Stars" to our resumes. I was in awe of how much this was going to change my life, and change the lives of those in my family.

I could actually buy a car now, an actual new car. Maybe I could buy my mom a new car too! I remember just dropping to my knees and thanking all of my angels, the universe, the Big Guy, and grandma too! I was almost "there," almost to the part where my hard work had paid off—almost. But I was always just 'almost' there. Now that I was at this place where life was going to change for the better, after working and waiting and working and waiting, how could there be anything other than "happily ever after"?

Oh silly girl, your optimism is adorable, don't ever lose it. There are two shoes and the other shoe hadn't dropped yet.

Chapter Fifteen

BUT SHE HAS A REALLY GREAT PERSONALITY

I could actually write a whole book about my experience with the TV show. There were so many twists and turns, behind the scenes drama, and even a villain or two. But mostly there were good people who impacted me profoundly. For now I'll put a pin in that book, until I see how the job search goes. For as life changing as that first phone call was, getting the news that we'd been picked up, the next phone call would be the exact opposite.

Well it would be life changing too, but more in the "carriage turns back into a pumpkin" way. We weren't doing a test run anymore, we were going to be a real TV show, so the finishing touches were being applied. It was more like fixing what wasn't broken but hindsight is 20/20.

My industry, the entertainment industry, is famous for fixing what isn't broken. It's an unfortunate reality. But studio execs were in charge now, and certainly they know what the people want, and it's usually the opposite of what the people are telling them they want.

We would begin filming in September to be ready for the fall lineup rollout, and between the current time and that moment, much needed to be done. It was during my summer vacation when I got word that one of the studio heads had an announcement to make, so we'd all need to be available for a conference call to share in the news.

It was slightly irritating for a few reasons. We all knew that a new morning show was being added. They were axing one of the shows from the test run and replacing them, hence the announcement. I don't think anyone was necessarily thrilled that a new show was coming on board, but mostly I wasn't thrilled with having to set my alarm on vacation so I could be on this call to feign excitement. I get three weeks a year to sleep in and I take that very seriously. There were more reasons for my irritation though. I would have loved nothing more than to be a cheerleader for the new addition, but I knew this spelled disaster for me.

I had a feeling, deep in my gut that this show was ultimately going to replace my show. A psychic once told me that we all have a little psychic intuition. Well I had tapped into my ability to see the future, and as I sat on this conference call, still in bed in my PJ's, sadness took over. No one ever intimated that my show would be taking a back seat, it was just one of those things you know.

The TV show concept still had the cameras bouncing back and forth between the four morning shows while we dished the daily celebrity news, and the sentiment was that everyone was equal and the funniest bits made it on to the show. I'd already learned during the test run that this wasn't really true. In true Detroit fashion, we were the underdog. We would get word from the editors that the funniest things done that day came from Detroit, but when we'd watch the show that evening Detroit had the least amount of airtime. The other shows would be featured doing the stories we nailed, crushed, and knocked out of the comedy ball park. It was hard, day after day, to see how many segments the other shows got versus how many Detroit got, and it was hard to ignore the reason why this "might" be happening.

It couldn't be because I wasn't the perfect size for TV could it?

The TV audience didn't care that I was bigger. I made them laugh, and that's what I was supposed to do. One of my TV colleagues had even singled me out. He's a famous actor, comedian, and syndicated radio personality—he's a big deal. He mentioned me on a few occasions while promoting the TV show. He liked me, he thought I was funny, and that's the very definition of "praise from Caesar."

So the reviews were in, and they were all good. What was the holdup? Give this girl her close up! The experience still nagged at me. Was it going to be that way again?

I tried to focus on all of the positives: we were asked back, we were one of the four shows, I was going to be on TV! I'd have to keep the faith, hope I'm wrong about the new show being added, and believe that the audience's opinion would matter.

That is who we're making this show for, right?

Don't you just want to hug me? My naivety is precious.

We spent the remainder of the summer promoting the show, doing interviews, flying to Los Angeles for photo shoots and promo shoots, and it was all coming together. Before long it was time to start filming the TV show. LA invaded the Fisher Building once again, but the vibe was different this time around.

That should have served as another sign of what was to come. Our little family unit, the team who worked so closely during the test run had been disassembled. Our cameramen Kevin and Ed weren't coming back this time, and I couldn't fight to keep my stellar makeup artist. Others involved wanted to replace her, and I was outnumbered. I knew I would never look that fabulous again. I was just hopeful that the new person would be able to fill in that bald spot on the right eyebrow. At least Jason was coming back. I couldn't imagine if we had lost him too, as he had become such a good friend and so important to this show. So there we were, a bit fractured but so ready to turn out one hell of a funny TV show.

I remember one of the phone calls with the studio heads where one of them said to me, "Your life is never going to be the same from this moment on." Thankfully I didn't begin my caviar diet right then, because I was just months away from my life being exactly the same. My heart would be a little more bruised, but exactly the same.

It didn't take long to notice that Detroit rarely appeared on the show, and by the third night it was pretty obvious that the newly added radio show was getting most of the airtime. I recall watching one of the episodes that first week and counting the new show in nine segments before you ever saw anyone else, and we were nearly 20 minutes into a half hour show before Detroit appeared at all.

By the end of the second week there was no denying what was happening. We were being buried at the end of the show, if we were even featured at all. It was humiliating. We were doing funny, entertaining stuff, every single day, often better than the other shows. (Well with the exception of Atlanta, they can't stop being funny.)

So this wasn't a content issue, and it wasn't a talent issue, so what issue could we be possibly be having? Oh wait, there was a fat girl on TV, and that was going to be a problem.

I couldn't ignore the elephant in the room, (no pun intended). Someone back at studio headquarters was struggling with my appearance. It didn't matter how funny I was, I wasn't suitable for TV.

"Isn't there a cave you could relocate to ma'am, where you won't nauseate the public?"

Okay, no one ever actually said that, but that sentiment was clear. So I cried every day—literally every day—which was a problem, as I didn't want to compromise the badass false eye lashes I loved wearing. I worked incredibly hard every morning to do a fantastic radio show, and to do a fantastic television show, and all of my hard work sat on the floor of the editing room.

Jason was beyond a field producer, he had his directives from LA, but he fought so hard for my show. He knew we were doing amazing things, not just because he was a friend, but because he was good at his job. The cameramen even commented how hard it was for them to not laugh during taping, but it just didn't matter.

After the show I'd get home, and Jason and I would talk on the phone. He'd give me pep talks, try to assuage my fears, and never even charged a therapist fee. I kept doing more things to my hair, adding more black to my wardrobe, but I still couldn't "act" smaller.

I don't think I've ever felt so bad about myself. I think I could have sucked it up though, if the TV show had been my only job. After all, the money was out of this world. TV money is like regular money on super steroids, and it could have made my life so much better. But it was really hard to have to explain to my wonderful, loyal, and supportive listeners why we were never on the show. I was supposed to be representing Detroit, showing America our swagger, but night after night there was very little, if any, Detroit.

I asked my audience daily to support the TV show, and they tuned in every night. It was a raw deal for everyone, and I hated that I couldn't deliver on my promise. The two head execs called during taping on the Tuesday before Thanksgiving. The reason for the call was to tell us they wanted to talk after the show. It was kind of odd. They could have just called AFTER the show, but maybe this was the Hollywood way. At that moment, I predicted that they were dumping us. What was coming was the dreaded "It's not you, it's me," conversation.

Everyone thought I was crazy! They weren't dumping us! "Stop the dramatics, Allyson." I do get accused of that often. I felt it with every fiber of my being though. I knew it was over. So after the show was done for the day, with just three of us in the room, including myself and Jason, we called the producers back.

And in a phone call that was less than 2 minutes long, we were off the show. We never even got a reason why. They called it a "hiatus" and said we'd revisit things in a couple of months. No, we were done. Even if they really meant we'd be back on the show in January, (and that was a big if) I was done on this end. I wasn't going to cry or feel bad about myself any more. I'm really awesome. I'm a good person, and I am damn good at my job! I'm sorry they couldn't see all of that because it wasn't in a size 2 package, but I was getting back to feeling good about myself, ASAP.

The kicker was that they expected us to still finish taping the rest of the week. Where else but in show business can you fire someone then ask if they'd still work the rest of the week? The crew, cameraman, and makeup artist, got paid by the day, so for that reason alone I finished the rest of the week. I didn't want these people who had also just lost their jobs to lose any more money, but boy was it a challenge to make jokes for the TV show that just dumped me.

So I was right, that call back in July forecasted doom, and the addition of the new show spelled the end for me. It's kind of ironic that I had been told by many behind the scenes that Detroit was instrumental in the show getting picked up, and now they were moving on without us.

Hey, glad I could help.

My radio audience was going to get an honest explanation. They'd been a part of this journey from the onset, and they'd also worked very hard for this show. So on that Friday, through many tears, we shared the news with the listeners—the whole sordid tale.

I don't know about other morning shows, but on mine, crying definitely had a place, and this particular morning there was plenty. We thanked our crew, the entire Detroit team, and said our goodbyes on the air. And like Dorothy to the scarecrow, I told Jason "I think I'll miss you most of all."

The story doesn't actually end there though, as the TV show would be in my life for a while. I really didn't realized how much the rest of the country had taken to this little radio show from Detroit, but our absence caused what one viewer described as a "social media avalanche."

For the next two months their social media sites were bombarded with angry messages over our dismissal, and surprisingly enough, those messages weren't coming from Detroit. Sure Detroit made their feelings known for a few weeks, but then they were done. They still had the radio show, we were still here. It was the rest of the country that relentlessly expressed their disappointment. Every state in the country, all of them, liked the Detroit show, and they wanted us back.

I completely understand Sally Fields Oscar speech now, "You

like me, you really like me." After feeling bad about myself for so long, I felt vindicated. The very people we were making the TV show for liked what I did, and didn't care that I didn't look like Gisele.

I'll always remember a comment I read in one of the trade magazines. A gentleman in California wrote, "I sure hope they didn't get rid of her because she was fat, cause homegirl was funny as hell." I hope he knows that homegirl is grateful from the bottom of her heart. My radio show suddenly had people tuning in daily from every corner of the good ole US-of-A.

In January I actually did hear back from the studio executives. I don't think they expected that kind of public backlash. And I don't think they ever intended to bring Detroit back from "hiatus" but now an offer was on the table.

They wanted my show back two weeks out of the month, to serve as a sort of rotating show. Two weeks a month of TV money is really hard to pass up. I could have paid off all of my bills, bought a much needed new car, and finally started one of those savings accounts I hear so much about, and hope to have someday.

But I couldn't set precedent that it was okay to treat me "less than." I couldn't go back to feeling worthless every day because I wasn't perfect. People probably don't walk away from TV shows, and I won't lie, it wasn't easy. But in a situation where I was an asset, a reason people laughed, I was actually looked at as some sort of blemish, and that wasn't okay.

I think Oprah said, "We teach people how to treat us." She's always saying smart stuff, and this is important advice. I don't ever want to teach anyone that it's okay to treat me second rate.

And when I start to think about the lost TV money, there's beer for that. That's important advice, too.

Chapter Sixteen

THE BEGINNING OF THE END

Things were gradually getting back to normal for the morning show. The remaining pieces of TV equipment were eventually removed from my studio and before long you couldn't tell that a TV show had taken center stage for the previous 2 years.

It was a painful breakup, but I had my first love, my radio show and my listeners, and we were stronger than ever with some new friends along for the ride. It was such a good feeling seeing the tweets and Facebook messages coming in from Texas, New Jersey, Florida, Virginia, (well you get it) listening to my show in real time. In other states, people were choosing my show in Detroit over their own local shows.

I felt so much pride over that.

The TV turmoil was over, but that didn't mean we were done with drama, not by a long shot. A new adventure was about to begin, compliments of new ownership.

The radio station sale was complete and we were now the property of a brand new company. Hold on tight everybody. Many of my coworkers long joked about my pampered existence through the years at this radio station. I really had worked only there during my career, and had been sheltered from many of the changes that had been happening in the radio industry. Most of my colleagues bounced around, working for different stations, and different companies. That's the typical radio resume.

During the Disney years it was just a constant red carpet lifestyle! Jobs were as plentiful as grapes in a bunch. We actually paid people 10 dollars an hour to sit in the studio answering phones for the air talent. Yep, every on air personality had their own "phone answerer," There was no answering your own telephones for these DJ's. The concept of one employee "wearing many hats" just didn't happen here. We had entire departments filled with people from the heads of the department, all the way down to the hourly and part time workers of said department. This radio station was full of life and full of employed people.

When the next company took over, it changed a little. Clearly the "being paid to answer phones" job was too good to last, but we maintained a healthy staff of people with round the clock on air talent, and fully staffed departments. So this was all I knew. It just makes sense that you're going to be a better business when you employ qualified talented people, and lots of them.

My Pollyanna radio world was about to be rocked, and I would be schooled very quickly as to how drastically the industry had changed since I'd entered this building. Eliminating positions was the name of the game now, whether you needed that employee or not. And the more money the employee made, the bigger the target on their head was. Forget about how long and hard they'd worked to finally achieve their salary, someone could do it cheaper, and it didn't matter if they were not as good. Something was brewing that would make "Black Monday" look like a rain soaked picnic. It was a new world in my beloved chosen profession, and I was going to get a front row view.

When the sale was official, and we became property of the new company, nothing happened immediately. It was that calm, almost pleasant weather that people cite right before a tornado hits. Everyone remained on high alert as we'd heard rumblings of how the new company operated, but we stayed optimistic. Maybe they would find no reason to make changes here. After all, Detroit was crushing it! Our ratings were through the roof, our revenue was unmatched, that's what it's all about right? Don't fix it if it ain't broken.

Many radio stations had been purchased in this sale; hundreds of stations, all across the country, and it started like a domino effect. The changes took place in the bigger markets first, and then moved station to station. We would read weekly news stories about massive layoffs happening at our sister/brother stations and we'd tally up the numbers of the employees who'd been "downsized" at each specific station. Then we would have the cutest conversations, naively discussing why it "needed" to happen there but would never happen here.

Maybe they had duplicate staff? Maybe they didn't have good ratings or weren't making any money? Maybe those changes were really for the best and would have nothing to do with us here in Detroit?

You just want to snuggle people when they are being that adorable.

I was holding out hope though, trying to convince my coworkers, and playing head cheerleader. "We're going to make it! We're going to be okay! The company will love Detroit! No layoffs here, anyway!" Rah, rah, siss boom bah!

Detroit's day finally arrived, we were the next domino in the path, and it was brutal! It was one of the most painful things, professionally, that I'd witnessed to date, and I was one of the lucky ones. It began at the start of the business day, around 8:30a.m. My show was still on the air. We got reports back to the studio, in a kind of play by play of what was happening out "there." One by one my coworkers, so many good friends, were being led to the slaughter.

Okay, I amped up the theatrics a bit, but it felt that way.

And every time a new report came in of who we'd lost, jaws would just drop. So and so got fired? But we need so and so, how can this be happening? There was no rhyme or reason to who was being let go. We were losing necessary air talent too. These were amazing, talented, important on air personalities, and we were not just losing THEM, but the positions were being eliminated completely!

No more night DJ's? No more overnight DJ's? But this is a major city, we need people on the air ALL the time. How will we continue to win this way?

I'd always been able to put the good face on any challenge, but it was hard to see a path to victory after we'd handicapped ourselves so permanently. And smack dab in the middle of it all was Ron. It had to be the last thing he ever wanted to do, but this was business, and these were his directives. Along with another high ranking manager from out of town, they spent the rest of the day firing people, in every single department. Necessary, talented people—people who worked hard and were damn good at their jobs, saw their positions eliminated. "Sorry we can't keep you any more, that position no longer exists here."

I don't profess to be a genius in the world of business, but it would seem that eliminating positions that are actually quite necessary to your business is counterproductive. I get it, paying people to answer phones for DJ's is a silly position, but no longer having a night jock, or an overnight jock, or midday jock, or weekend help, or producers, or support staff in all of the departments? Just one person is going to be a department now? How can this make us better?

I know the cuts weren't intended to make us better, even Pollyanna over here understands "cost-cutting measures", but it seems there will be an ultimate price to pay for this logic. A rush of cash now, and then what later? A really smart man, probably Benjamin Franklin, once said "You have to spend money to make money."

I think that guy was on to something.

I left right after my show that day. I was out the door the minute the mic light turned off. The next day we could feel the emptiness. It was like a ghost town. I could almost envision tumbleweeds rolling through. Those of us fortunate enough to still have jobs moved forward. We smiled, thanked our lucky stars, and did our best to assimilate into this new culture. We were a smaller group now, but still had the same work to do. We had to keep this radio station number one, to keep my morning show number one, and regardless of what limitations we faced, we would not stop kicking ass!

More challenges and hurdles would come as time went on in the typical growing pains of becoming property of a new company. The "downsizing" was in our rear view mirror, but there would be more upheaval before long. Many of the people who'd made the cut were finding it hard to acclimate to our new normal, and another wave of coworkers was making the decision to leave, this time voluntarily. Our much smaller family was busting apart at the seams, and really important people were choosing to move on. I was trying so hard to convince people to stay, to keep this powerhouse of people together, but my friends, my teammates, had gone as far as they could under the new guidelines. We were about to lose the world's best midday guy, the world's best afternoon guy, the wonderful woman in traffic who'd kept this place on point for decades, not to mention, THE BEST sales people in the business. These were monster sales people—you know the kind that can sell ice to a freezer? All of these key people had contributed to making this radio station number one, and now one after another they were walking out the door.

And Pollyanna here still thought we could win. I was not throwing in the towel. I'd worked too hard—we'd worked too hard. My heart was breaking again. We'd lost the first batch of important people in the firings, and now we had lost the rest. The toughest pill to swallow was coming though, and there would be no lying to myself that we'd survive this. By the way, for those keeping track, this really IS the entertainment industry, where laughs and smiles lead the way. ;)

It was after my show one morning with a few of us in my studio discussing the next day's show, when Ron entered the room. He'd come in to share some news, and you could feel immediately that this wasn't going to be show or station related. Then came the words I'd been dreading, that we'd all been dreading. He was going to be leaving us. He was stepping down from his position at this radio station. It was a shock, but we'd kind of seen it coming.

We'd seen how many new "hats" Ron was wearing and it was taking its toll. Ron's priorities are family and faith first. Of course he kills it professionally, the proof is in the pudding, but too much was being asked. I think most of us knew this could possibly happen, but we all just prayed that somehow it wouldn't.

We only have one head, perfect for our one specialized hat. Who was the idiot that developed the business model where one worker wears 56 hats at the same time, all the time? We should find that guy and give him some what for.

(Side bar: Possibly the greatest of all the old timey sayings? I've never understood it, but my grandpa wanted to dole out "what for" regularly.)

Tears flowed immediately, as Ron's leaving was going to impact the station profoundly, like in a "we probably won't make it" kind of way. It also hurt personally. Here was another person I cared about who was leaving, a person who took good care of the radio station that mattered so much to me.

Most people aren't tripping over themselves to leave number one radio stations, so they might've wanted to re-evaluate things, I'm just sayin'. Ron was leaving a number one radio station. He'd turned this place into a force in this market, a station that others were trying to duplicate. All eyes were on us. I know this decision wasn't an easy one to make, as he had so many reasons to stay, but like all of the others piling out the door before him, something had to give. I'd survived a lot of shakeups in the past 16 or 17 years, but this was a big one. Almost everyone was gone now. Everyone that contributed to the success of this station—gone.

That just left the morning show, the only constant at a radio station that had gone through so much change. It was the last of what was familiar for the audience. I was going to do everything I could to keep fighting for the station, and fighting for my show.

When was the fighting going to stop though? Why was there always some sort of battle?

I guess when you care about something, maybe that's what it feels like. Maybe not everyone gets emotionally involved when stations get decimated, but I can't understand that level of detachment. I think our time is better spent valuing, appreciating, contributing, and enjoying, but this is a business of egos and more egos, so a lot of time gets wasted on that silliness.

So my uphill journey had just gotten a little more uphill. What else is new? This had been the theme of my career from the onset. And it's true, I had many new challenges in front of me now, but I'd been there before. I am definitely an army of one, so I knew I was going to meet these challenges head on with a plan to be victorious. But I also knew that people matter, and it was going to be much harder now to stay number one by myself.

At least the earth wasn't scorched yet, so that was something right? The earth wasn't scorched YET Allyson, but soon I would meet some A1 scorchers, who specialize in "nothing ever grows here again."

I had to remind myself, "Allyson, not everyone cares as much about this place as you do, and not everyone is interested in your show staying number one."

Soon I'd find out how much of an army of one I really was.

Chapter Seventeen

ONE SMOOOOOV NEGOTIATOR

The day that nobody was looking forward to finally arrived. It was Ron's last day. He didn't have that last minute change of heart I had been praying for. This was the very last day he would be our program director, and it was definitely tough. I had been through this so many times before with PD's coming and going, but this loss was going to have a lasting ripple effect. There was an ominous feeling in the air, like we'd just dislodged the wrong giant Jenga tile, and the whole station was about to come toppling down.

Ron's last day at the radio station was a bizarre day. For me especially, there were so many moving parts to it, and last minute surprises. We did not just have the sad task of saying goodbye to our leader and friend, we would also be meeting new people that day, as the new owners were making their first visit to the station. Ron was leaving and it was a good time to learn all about this number one rated station from the man who had gotten us there.

People walked on eggshells and hoped to keep a low profile, as these were the big deal leaders of this company. COCOOs and VIPs and CEOs and one of the actual owners.

One bad elevator conversation and who knows what could happen?

The best advice given that day was to smile and be helpful to anyone in a sharp looking suit. At that time, I was coming to the end of a 5 year contract. It was up in about a month, and I was still deciding whether or not to get an agent. I'd hired an agent once before and got burned, and through the years on my own I got burned, so I didn't have a good track record. To date, in this long illustrious career I've had, the very first contract I signed in 1995 to do overnights remains the fairest deal I've ever signed.

At this moment, I held all the cards. My morning show was number one in numerous demo's, and had been for years. We'd had the TV show, and I was the catalyst that took the morning show to number one. During my tenure, on two occasions I'd turned struggling morning shows into highly rated morning shows, so I could add that to my "cool things about me" list. But having this power was lost on me, and I didn't know how to wield it. Frankly that side of the business makes me very uncomfortable. I don't think it's fun to negotiate. I just think if you have a valuable employee, and you're making a lot of money because of their hard work, you should pay them the going rate for what it is they do.

Now you can see why I'd received so many bad deals over the years. I was waiting for others to just do the right thing and give me a fair share. Honestly, in the world I live in, it's a perfectly normal way to do business. I also didn't like the idea of getting an agent and talking "through" someone. That doesn't seem like the best way to get to know each other. I want us to be friends, to care about each other. We'll achieve better results that way, right?

Clearly I was still struggling with this decision. I sure wish I knew Gloria Allred. But this wasn't something I planned to deal with that day. That day was about saying goodbye to Ron, and staying out of the way of important business dealings. After all we hadn't received any word that our presence was requested during this corporate visit, and no meetings had been set up between us, so staying out of the way seemed appropriate.

It's a double edged sword. On one side you want them to want to meet you, and to think you are important enough to have a chat with. On the other side, it's just an opportunity to say the wrong thing with caraway seeds in your teeth to the person who now owns you. It's hard to know which to root for.

On a soon to be understood, related note, I looked particularly stunning on this day. That's a trick I can pull off when I receive prior confirmation in email form that important people will be walking through my work area. Without the friendly heads up, I would most likely plow into Mr. BigWig Von Quarterly sporting spaghetti stained pajama pants and a bun wrapped with a scrunchie.

I'm a chameleon in that way.

I was getting close to calling it a day. My morning show had been over for a while, and if no one needed me it would just be awkward I f I continued to stick around. So I went looking for Ron, as it was time for the part of the day I had been dreading. It was time to say goodbye. And I'd drink in one long last look at this radio station the way it should be, with Ron in charge. Starting the next day, a new journey that terrified my soul would begin. I was in no way shape or form giving up, but I'm a realist, and now this boat had a lot of holes in it. I made my way to his office and found it packed to the gills with corporate. It was like a suit convention at the suit warehouse. It was like a suit explosion in a—okay I'm done. But here I was getting a glimpse of some of the new company faces. I met the VP of something, and the COCOO of something else, and I'm sure there was an acquisitions guy, because that would make sense.

At that moment Ron was busy, but one of the gentlemen asked if I could take him to an office on the 8th floor. I happily obliged. And as I was leaving, Ron quickly told me to make sure I came right back, because the owner of the company wanted to meet with me. The communications business is funny, in that we're not really great at it, and sometimes you get your important information just like that.

My day had just changed on a dime—good call on not wearing the spaghetti stained pajama pants.

The owner wanted to see me? He wanted to see me? Did he want to see anyone else affiliated with the morning show? Ron told me that he just wanted to meet with me.

I was mentally preparing for this impromptu meeting, and trying not to over analyze it. Of course it couldn't be bad, why would it be? Everything within me told me it was going to be fine, but after the months of loss we'd just experienced I was still a little shell-shocked.

I delivered my corporate guy to his destination and rounded my way back towards Ron's office. They were all on a break now, and Ron was actually coming down the hallway, and I realized this was it. I probably wouldn't get another chance to see him, and I was overcome with tears. It was time to say goodbye. I knew that when I came to work the next morning he wouldn't be there anymore.

I hugged him goodbye one last time, and then he let me know the owner would be discussing my contract with me. He asked me if I was ready for that, and I knew what he meant. He was asking me if I was going to be able to handle myself. He knew my deals had been less than stellar and I know he wanted better for me. I was as ready as I would ever be. If this was happening today, let's do this! Ron gave me this look that said "Be strong and take care of you up there," and I wiped away tears as I stepped on to the elevator for the 8th floor conference room.

This has to be the very definition of closing one chapter and beginning another. It was so surreal—goodbye/hello. Still trying to pull it together, I was relieved when I entered the conference room and the new owner wasn't there yet. I had a little more time to compose. Normally a person doesn't go into this type of meeting on the heels of a good crying jag.

Our conference room held a very large table. It takes up the entire room—it's almost presidential. The owner had set up camp at the head of the table on the other side of the room so I grabbed the chair directly to the left of him. I patiently began waiting for him to arrive, and tried to imagine how this would go down.

"So you own hundreds of radio stations huh? That must be fun, would you like to see pictures of my cats?"

Maybe I wouldn't lead with that, but I was actually looking

forward to it at that point, and not feeling nervous at all. One of my strong skills is being able to talk to anyone about anything. I don't often get intimidated. We're all people right? We're all deserving of respect with no reason to ever feel "less than" anyone else. So why not get in there and mix it up?

I couldn't help but notice all of the pieces of paper and the files that had all been splayed out in front of his chair. Was that my entire history? Was everything I'd ever done in little piles for his perusal? I didn't have to occupy myself with wondering and imagining for long as he finally entered the room. We are prepared for liftoff Allyson, are you ready to be charming as hell?

Child, please.

I immediately stood up to meet him as he walked toward his chair, and we each extended our hands toward the other for a good firm shake. He had a warmth about him, and a very nice smile, and whether or not he really was pleased to meet me, he definitely made me feel that way. He was also very charismatic and handsome as long as we're noticing things. He sat down and proceeded to go over my history, being extremely complimentary about my talent and my accomplishments. I almost felt like he'd been following my career, as he seemed to have such an intimate knowledge about me, and he appeared to be impressed.

Well this was great, if he already thinks I'm awesome, and he wouldn't be wrong, than the long future I wanted with his company was in the bag!

It was just a very nice conversation, and although I was never prepared to have it that day, or even have it myself, it was going really well. I believe the universe was stepping in again, and intervening on my behalf. If I hadn't been caught off guard, maybe I would have gotten an agent, and I wouldn't have had this chance to make an impression. What I wanted most was longevity; it's always been my main goal. I wanted to work for a very long time, and I wanted the people I work for to know that they have the best they can get.

As for money, I just felt like it would come. Now here comes the part of our meeting that subjected me to ridicule from coworkers for quite a while. I'm honest when I talk. I don't know any other way to be. If I tried to "play the game" it would be awkward and clumsy and most people know me to be smoov, with a V, always. So I talked from the heart, and I told this man what was truly important to me, I said "I'm not motivated by money, I'm motivated by loyalty."

Anyone I shared that with told me I was plain stupid for saying that in a negotiation. I just think that if I was in his chair, I'd want to know that someone who worked for me felt loyalty was important. Regardless, I spoke the truth. I'm the girl who turned down triple her salary to go to a crosstown radio station, a competitor. What would that have done to the people I cared about here? Or the radio station I love? Or my audience? So now I'm dividing the listeners? I believed that an offer to triple my salary would come back around again. I'm really good at what I do, but I have to be able to sleep at night too.

It may come back around someday but not that day. He asked me point blank what I wanted, and I said it—the words came right out of my mouth, "I want my salary doubled." Sure, it may sound amazing to have your salary doubled, but for who I was, and all I'd done, and what my salary was currently? Let's just say that an agent might have had a stroke at that moment…actually would have, *would have* had a stroke.

I wanted this man to get to know me, to see firsthand how valuable I am. So I took that deal believing that the future had wheelbarrows full of money in it for me. I was in this for the long haul. I'm young, I'm at the top of my game, and I'll be working until I'm Barbara Walters' age. I left feeling good about things. Sure my boyfriend was going to blow a gasket, and for the next five years I wouldn't be in the same financial stratosphere as my peers. That's the hard pill, but I was going to be a star in the company.

Looking back I wouldn't have changed anything about that day, although there was information to which I was not privy. Apparently four horsemen had been dispensed from across the galaxy, and were headed this way. I think things absolutely would have worked out as I envisioned, I just hadn't factored in the evil. We really need an app for that, an "evil calculator."

Oh and it was coming, like dark storm clouds that gather in the Midwest—it was coming.

Chapter Eighteen

GOING DOWNHILL IS ONLY FUN WHEN SLEDDING

So here we were in an all too familiar place, about to embark on a brand new beginning at the radio station. Obviously, this wasn't a new feeling at all. I mean at this point in my career I couldn't remember all the people who had passed through these hallways. Constant changes were actual very normal, but there was something that was different this time. In the past there was always something to hold on to, something to build on. Bigger pieces of the station remained versus the smaller pieces, i.e whatever current change we were experiencing.

But not this time. It was like for the first time in 20 years this place had been scrubbed spotless, cleaned and disinfected sterile. Normally my position is that you can never have too much Clorox Clean-Up. I'm a huge fan, but it almost felt like it had been used here. The history, the heart, the burnt on flakes of spice and "flava" were gone.

What were we going to build on? And who was left that loved this place?

I'd been at that radio station my entire adult life. I grew up there, and I loved that place, the way you love a childhood home, or grandma's house—a special dwelling that holds so many cherished memories.

I was protective of this radio station. I knew it inside and out. Whose hands its fate was in mattered to me. It was my business. Was the person taking over yet again going to care about this place, and the employees? Would they have a strong desire to win with the talent to back it up? I was feeling less and less optimistic about the answer to that question. But I never give up, because who knows? I held out hope that I could be pleasantly surprised. I even convinced myself that this could be the greatest chapter of the stations history yet!

Yep, I'm that girl. I can see white flags waving, ships sinking, locusts swarming, and think, "This is great! We still have a chance to win!"

Winning was still my plan.

I was about to sign a new five year deal, and at that moment in time the radio station and my morning show were #1. #1, #1, #1—it's an important statistic to remember. After the new owner returned home to corporate land, he and his attorney sent me a copy of my new contract. I was so excited to be signing another long term contract there, and he'd gotten it back to me so quickly. Now I just needed to scan it, sign it, and send it back.

Damn technology! Now I had to find someone to teach me how to scan. When did we stop faxing things?

I was still receiving playful jabs from the coworkers I'd shared my contract details with, but I was fine with my choices. I had long term plans. I was currently getting three weeks vacation. At almost twenty years, it sure felt like I should at least get four, so I quickly emailed back that I'd like four weeks of vacation.

The lawyer promptly responded that it wasn't doable, but before her email even hit the inbox the owner replied back "Make it so."

Well he just agreed to the four weeks, but how many extra cool points would he have gotten for "Make it so." ?

Within two days of our surprise meeting, I was officially signed to the new company! I would be getting double my salary, four weeks of vacation a year and employment for the next five years. Regardless of how cold it seemed at the station, I was looking at all of the positives. I remained tireless in my quest to keep us on top, and maintain a family atmosphere. T's were crossed, and i's were dotted as available positions were secured. I even intervened with a recommendation for someone I thought would be an asset. Why not?

I sent an email up the corporate ladder and used my "clout" to place a vote for who I thought could help my show stay the course. It appeared to have worked as the person I recommended for the job did in fact get it, however helping me and my show was the last thing she had planned. It wouldn't be long until her sights were set on seeing me out the door.

I never would have imagined that in the not so distant future, she would get her wish. Why would this company that signed me to a 5 year deal, this company that knows how valuable I am and how hard I'd worked to make the morning show successful ever give clearance for such a petty personal move? I felt safe in the notion that they wouldn't, so I continued to stand up for myself and the radio station. After all, I had our best interests at heart.

Through the years there were several people I helped in this manner. I'd saved someone's job, I gave someone a job, and I used my status to help someone else get a job.

In every one of those cases, it bit me in the behind.

My boyfriend finally asked me if I'd learned a lesson about helping people. My answer was no, I hadn't learned any lessons. I wasn't going to change who I am because of unfortunately crossing paths with some unscrupulous people.

This is the business I work in. If you don't have the actual skill or talent, you find other ways to make it to the top.

I got blindsided on three pretty brutal occasions, but I focus on all of the interns I'd mentored, or colleagues that I'd helped along the way. I was proud that I was able to help people get jobs, or get their foot in the door. That's what we're supposed to do. Three times it was ugly, but the other 97% of the time it was fulfilling, and I was for others what a few select radio heroes were for me.

I guess I'd tell my boyfriend that I learned not to let the ugliness of some people keep me from paying it forward to the rest. (Yeah, that's a good one, I need to remember to tell him that later.)

After this person began plotting, things seemed to immediately start falling apart around the station. But like a good soldier, I started firing off emails, doing everything I could to rally the troops. We had a really fantastic lead there, and we needed to work to keep it. More than a year had gone by at this point, and I convinced myself things were great, but it was a hard sell.

I knew what kind of effort was being put forth, but I couldn't have expected what came next. It was a day that floored me, with news that just broke my heart.

During the year and a half that followed our being purchased, our ratings had plummeted. The morning show was no longer #1 in any demo, and in the demo that we'd remained untouchable in for years, we'd fallen to 4th place. No one in the past year and a half ever revealed that information to the morning show. The entire time we were falling out of our lead, we were never shown our ratings. We still thought we were #1.

We were actually still running promo's on the air thanking Detroit for making us #1 in the morning!

It was humiliating. All of the hard work put in for so many years had been squandered with no one uttering a peep.

As heartbroken as I was, surprised I was not. I had been constantly rattling the cage, as I knew we weren't doing enough. I knew we weren't doing anything, and my objections always landed on deaf ears. It was hard to ignore the fact that maybe the morning show failing was part of the plan. They had policies put into place that kept people from talking to each other, or working together, and the last station meeting we had was back in the Ron days.

I used to hate meetings, but I'd spent the last year and a half begging for them. I would have given anything for one of those useless meetings that caused my eyes to roll. I mean we were in a bit of a crisis, it couldn't hurt to all sit in a room and talk to each other, right? Add pizza even—we'll call it a pizza party! We'll do whatever it takes to form a game plan. Why didn't everyone share my concerns?

Clearly the new company wasn't going to be happy with this new turn of events, and a few of us realized that we had to get word to them about what was or wasn't happening here. But how do you even go about that? How do you contact your new owners and broach this conversation?

We'd convinced ourselves that they would be able to see where the holes were, and they'd figure it out. We'd just have to wait for that.

And we thought we might just want to add praying to the mix, too.

More time went by and people started curiously losing their jobs. We finally reached out to a couple of high ranking officials, some who were in the building and some very high up the company ladder. We had to share our concerns.

This house plant was intentionally being denied water! We just need a water can! Someone please send water! When you're talking to VP's in circular talk, it's hard to get the message across. You just kind of hope they know what you're "trying" to say. Even as my legacy was being tarnished, I still wasn't necessarily trying to get anyone in trouble.

There was some real "deep throat" stuff going on at this time.There were secret meetings in hot parking garages, or stairwells on different floors. So many people were reaching out to whomever they could find. There was just not much more to do, but hope for the best and hope that all we'd built and had become would get us through this bizarre time. Things were going to play out the way they were going to play out.

In the meantime, 4th place or not, I went in every day and gave the show of my life. During those 4 1/2 hours life was beautiful. It was a damn good morning show, and we were blessed with an amazing audience, so I focused on that. Oh, and I went home and made a vision board, as I was definitely in need of some help from the universe. It had been a while since the powers that be gave me an assist, and at this point I was looking everywhere. I even hung a rosary next to my bed. I knew Grandma would really like that move.

It all kind of sounds like a made for the SyFy network movie where demon sharks terrorize a radio station, but it wasn't far off. (Note to self: approach Ian Ziering about possible script idea.)

I was focusing on the positives as I was about to celebrate my 20th anniversary at this wonderful radio station. It was a huge milestone, and I was really proud. I did that! I worked hard and I accomplished that! That was all me!

We were in need of all the attention we could get so the plan was to use my anniversary to possibly get some exposure for the radio station and for the morning show. So we'd send out a press release, and maybe get some of our TV friends to cover it. A little media attention, we thought, could do us good.

As we began putting together a plan for my anniversary tribute we were told to abort the mission. "No one is really interested in this sort of thing," was the quote. "Don't use the show to make a big deal out of this."

Wait, we're trying to get attention for all of us! We're dying on the vine here, so shouldn't we use any opportunity we have to get our call letters out there, and get exposure for the station?

This was when I was the most adorable—when giant red flags that flash warning wave right in front of my face. They scream, "Allyson pay attention to this. This is not a normal response to a beloved morning host's milestone! There is danger ahead, danger!!"

And on the morning of July 13th, 2015 we took a whopping 2-3 minutes to acknowledge my accomplishment. I swept the last red flag under the carpet where I'd been keeping the others, and I just kept moving, unaware that those four horsemen were getting closer to Detroit.

And I still hadn't started one of those savings accounts I'd always heard so much about. That's okay, I was only two years into my new 5 year contract.

I had plenty of time.

Plenty of time.

Chapter Nineteen

AND KINDNESS CAME FROM EVERYWHERE

Dear Allyson,

I moved back to Michigan from Florida in 2007 when I was going through a divorce and I discovered you on the radio and I was hooked and listened every am. I would even stream you in when I went out of town to get my fix. I loved your sense of humor and I pretty much have the same values and morals you do. I always agreed with your side. I love how you share about Warren and your relationship. I love your kitty stories as I have 3 of my own. Had 5 when I moved here. I share your love of animals. I feel like you were such a big part of my day. You would make me LOL when I was down in the dumps and made me feel better. I felt a connection. Im still in shock about what happened, I don't understand how anyone could let you go. I won't listen anymore. I tried listening and it just wasn't the same. I will miss you so much. I hope someone else scoops you up, and realizes what a gem you are. I know this is a very hard time for you, but know you have made a special place in my life and many others. You are not just a voice but a comfort and I feel lost not hearing you. I know with Warren and the kitties you will have comfort. Things will work out for you, but you have to go through this to get to where you are going. Sending you love and hugs xoxox

Connie

I'd never seen anything like it, it was dizzying, and it was almost non-stop. Never in my wildest dreams could I have imagined this unbelievable show of kindness and support. I had just had everything taken from me. All that I had worked for was ripped from my life, and these blessings too numerous to count came pouring into my inboxes at a rapid pace, each one just as thoughtful as the next.

My heart had been shattered due to this blindside, yet constant comfort kept wrapping around me. I remember thinking "I never got to say goodbye," and wondered what it would feel like not being able to speak to you/my listeners, my friends, anymore. And as fast as these feelings were filling me, almost on cue I would get an answer to a question I had just asked myself. It was as if everyone could read my mind, and were feeling the same way.

At first I couldn't wrap my brain around just how many messages were coming through, I had to take a step back to get my bearings, but within a month I began to read, and read, and read. And then I printed. Maybe it sounds silly, but I printed every single one of those notes. I stopped printing when I hit the 3,000th message, because my boyfriend wouldn't allow me to use anymore printer paper. (Something about not having a job anymore and printer paper not growing on trees. He was clearly using my weakened state to try to be the boss of me.)

There would be more messages, as they continued to come, I even answered some today, but I carried around that stack of 3,000 messages as if it were a security blanket.

When I started to panic or feel like maybe I wasn't strong enough for this, I'd just leaf through and find the most loving words. I would get online in the middle of the night, now that the alarm clock was out of a job, and I just stayed up all night long responding to each and every message. I needed every single person who'd taken the time to care about my current loss to know just what their words meant to me. I don't know how many people get lucky enough to feel kind arms around them at their lowest, but there isn't enough gratitude in the world to allow me to fully and properly express my feelings.

I experienced an avalanche of emotions that led to falling apart

What do I do now? Who am I now? What happens to me next?

Utter fear.

I'd always taken care of myself, and worked hard so I could provide, not just for me, but now for my family too. Timing being as perfect as always, I'd just began helping my family through their own losses.

What will happen to all of us? How will I take care of us all?

In many of the messages I received, people shared with me their own struggles of similar experiences, and offered advice. One woman told me she'd had almost the identical thing happen to her and she understood the feeling of devastation. Within five months she'd found a better job at better pay, so it wound up being the best thing that ever happened to her. She said if she could go back and do anything differently she would have enjoyed those five months she was out of work and encouraged me to embrace this time, as it would definitely be short lived.

I loved that advice!

It involved kicking back, and having fun, and I sure gave it the old college try. I went to the pool, and got together with friends, but the worry never left.

With everything on the line it was just too hard to Carpe that Diem. And our normally roomy apartment felt much smaller now. I was doing all I could to not cramp Warren's space too much. This had become his primary workplace over the years, and now with both of us home every single day, the potential for stir crazy was at maximum.

After an emergency, self-run, couple's therapy session, we were able to avoid potential destruction. It turns out excessive vacuuming can actually be cited as a primary reason for breaking up.

Phew, thankfully we caught it in time.

And then I started to plan for the worst, because the worst was all I could think of. Despite my new battle cry, "The best is yet to come," until the best got here I would continue to have constant flashes of panic.

I was determined, however, not to give in to anger. I wasn't going to let it eat at me. I wasn't looking back or spending one second thinking about those who'd wronged me. I needed my whole self to stay positive and stay focused and not let the ugliness consume me.

What a blessing it was to find that strength. I can't imagine how much harder things would have been if I hadn't been able to let go of it with such ease, because normally I can grudge it up with the very best of them.

Sleepless nights were becoming pretty familiar. On cue my brain would decide the best time to worry about everything was at the very time I was ready for sleep. What makes the brain do that? Shouldn't we be working together? Come on cerebellum, we're supposed to be a team!

It was on one of those sleepless nights when I started developing back up plans, preparing for absolute catastrophic conditions, and wondering if necessary did I have what it took to be a phone sex operator?

I mean they seem to make good money, and they work from home! I reached over to grab the stack of messages lying in a pile next to me on the bed. I wasn't kidding when I said I kept them close to me.

Warren very much needed sleep, and my tossing and turning, and TV blaring the ID Network all night made that a challenge for him, so he was often sleeping on the couch.

Someone has to be rested for work around here.

On that particular night, I once again started reading, and reading, and reading. I was almost like a detective going over a crime scene in search of clues that might have been previously overlooked. (See? A LOT of ID Network.)

All of a sudden something clicked. I could almost physically feel a click, and I instantly started to smile. My brain finally shut up with the, "Will your phone sex job pay our bills?" questions, and I began to feel more positive than I'd felt in years.

And before that night, or morning, (whatever it was at this point) before it was over, I felt like I was the luckiest person in the world.

I couldn't explain this surge of optimism that was over taking me. I mean, my situation hadn't changed. I went from making a list of things I could sell to making a list of things I was going to buy. I was making big, grand plans for my future, starting with a first class trip to Disney World. As I re-read the messages, the beautiful words jumped off the page in a brand new way.

Then it hit me—how could all of these people be wrong?

They were all saying the same thing. And they cared enough to make sure I knew all the reasons why I would be okay. Actually, according to them, I was going to be better than okay. Every note, message, email, they all had almost identical sentiments, "This will be the best thing that ever happened to you." Thousands of people who didn't know each other were all telling me the same thing.

So how could I NOT be okay?

How could the best NOT be coming?

That's far too many people to all be wrong. I knew who I was. I was the same person who'd built a successful morning show several times. I was a radio personality at the top of my field, and the very best at what I do. Somebody's intentional bad judgement doesn't change who I am, what I've done, or what is next for me.

And at that moment I let go, and it was like being carried down a stream. I was feeling excited about what the future was holding for me. One message made me giggle, as she summed it up this way, "Allyson, send them a thank you card RIGHT NOW! I think we're feeling sorry for the wrong person, you don't need our support, you will be amazing!"

And my sleepless nights stopped after that night.

Chumbawamba once said, "I get knocked down, but I get up again, you're never gonna keep me down."

And they were right. (They were kind of the Socrates of the 90's.)

There is no way to prevent the rug from getting yanked out on a random Monday blindside—we just haven't developed an app for that yet.

But what we do next, how we define ourselves, how we move forward— only we get to make that choice.

I choose to be awesome, and unwavering, and better than I ever imagined I could be. It's funny, right around this time each year I'd start dreading the arrival of snow. For someone who loves where she lives you'd think I'd have made my peace with winter. But I'm not a fan, not at all. It started decades ago when I was new at the radio station, and I tangled with some black ice coming home from my overnight shift.

After doing three complete spins mid expressway, I smashed into the side of the concrete wall, cracking the frame of my boyfriend's shiny new Volkswagen Scirocco. (Cherry Red.) Oh was he heartbroken. The good fortune I received from the universe, from my angels, or my grandma kept an 18 wheeler from hitting the same patch and pinning me into the wall. So yeah, I've got a beef with you, winter. You started it!

Every year I dread winters return and immediately go into whine mode. "I don't want to drive in the snow. Stupid snow, I wish I didn't have to leave in the snow." Anytime it snowed on a day I didn't have to work I'd say, "Hahaha, you didn't get me winter." (I probably should be ashamed to admit that I get into verbal spats with seasons, yet [illegible] not so much.)

It snowed early this year and I looked out my window with a

different thought this time. I wanted so much to be getting ready to head out into the snow, to make that commute I could drive blindfolded, after so many years of taking that same route. I never thought I'd actually want to tackle the icy roads, but to get to my studio? To get to my morning show? I was feeling that now. I wanted to be driving in this snow.

It's been some time now since I've been able to say through a microphone "Good Morning, Detroit", but it won't be forever.

And until I can get back in my car and drive through the snow to get to the place where I say it again, for now I'm still a message away.

I'll be back and doing great things soon. Nothing's going to keep me down.

To my listeners, I love you and miss you, and I'm working my way back to you as fast as I can. Stay tuned, there's much more to come with my life on air!

AND IT WOULDN'T BE A BOOK BY ALLYSON WITHOUT THIS: KITTIES I HAVE LOVED

The following are the stories of a few of the kitties that my radio listening family have come to know over the years. My fur babies are a huge part of the love I have experienced and given in my life, and so I want to share some of their stories here. If any of these stories inspire you, maybe you'd like to donate to a no-kill shelter near you, or maybe you'll just be inspired to go to one and adopt a baby of your own. Either way, it just wouldn't be a book by Allyson without some kitties in it!

ROSIE

Rosie was found on Roosevelt Rd. in Chicago. My mom's boyfriend at the time worked in road construction, and found this tiny little creature one day amidst the broken concrete. I was 11 years old when Rosie came to live with us, and she'd be in my life for the next 18 years. She made the trip to Michigan when we relocated from Chicago. My mom loaded up a station wagon with her two daughters, all of our worldly possessions, and our two cats Rosie and Big Cat. They rode in the car like people—no carriers for them. It was the late 70's/early 80's, so safety was not the name of the game yet.

In Rosie's final years she came to live with Warren and I in our apartment. We called it her retirement home. She'd been allowed to go outside once we moved to Michigan, but now that she was older those days were over. I had just started working overnights at the radio station in Detroit, and on the nights I was gone, Warren would tuck Rosie into his jacket and walk her around the complex.

It was a little taste of what she didn't get to have any more. We are advocates of cats being strictly kept inside, but things were different back in the 80's when she had full reign of the outdoors. Rosie lived with us for close to two years when she succumbed to kidney failure. When we finally had to help her across the rainbow bridge, we both held her paws as she went to sleep. Rosie lived an exciting, globetrotting 18 years, and was an important member of our family. We love you big girl!

ROSWELL

Roswell is Rosie's namesake. After Rosie passed, Warren and I decided we were ready to start our own fur family, so we went in search of our "first born." I wanted a kitten, (who doesn't?) but it was important to us that we picked the cat that needed us the most. That's when we met "Jack in the Box." The rescue named him that because he never came out of his box! He was the scaredest little boy ever. He was about 9 to 11 weeks old when we met him, and we knew right away that he needed a family, so we walked past the nursery to Jack in the Box's cage, and he became our Roswell that day.

Roswell never let me hold him in all of his 17 years, but that was okay, all I wanted was for him to be happy and loved. And he was, and he loved his dad so much! He thought that guy hung the moon. He never really got over being scared, but he had a great life filled with brothers and sisters, parents who loved him and a toy basket to be jealous of. We used to say "Roswell never does anything wrong," because he was always such a good boy, and he was the best big brother. Roswell lived to be 17 years old. We still love and miss our biggest boy.

MARLEY

Oh, Marley was a special one! You never want your "kids" to think you have favorites but Marley was something else. His dad actually referred to him as "my special little guy". Marley was a magical creature who was part panda bear and part bunny rabbit—at least in the story I used to tell him. We felt that we should get a mate for Roswell, because we thought it would help him adjust and feel more comfortable. About 6 months after Roswell joined our family, we went back to the shelter in search of a baby girl, and I already had her name picked; Maggie. (I might have gotten it from the Simpsons—it's possible.)

We went into the nursery to look at the babies as they all came piling out of a cage. The very last one was tripping over herself to keep up with the others. "She" was 3 weeks old, and was the tiniest thing I'd ever seen! She was all head. She had a broken tail, so that was the final sign that she was meant to be ours. They almost didn't let us take her

home that day because of how small she was, but since we'd just gotten Roswell from the same place they made an exception.

I had to run back home to grab a kitty carrier, and while I was gone people kept asking Warren if they could hold her. She literally fit in the palm of his hand. He finally had to start turning people away. This was his baby, now. But that's how special this little one was. Everyone wanted to hold her. I returned and we proceeded to check out, when at the very last minute we were told they had made a mistake, Maggie was actually a boy!

So they asked if we wanted to put him back and get a girl, and oh my goodness, I can't even imagine. In that short span of time we already loved that little baby with all of our hearts, so Maggie became Marley. Because he was so tiny he had to spend the first week in our bedroom closet. I was so afraid something would fall on him. It wasn't long until Roswell figured out how to break him out of that joint though. That was his baby, and he wanted him. They would be brothers and friends for many years to come. Losing Marley was a tough one. We thought we'd have more time, but we didn't. What we did have was 17 loving years with one of the coolest cats anyone ever met. Mama and Papa love you special little guy!

PHOEBE

Phoebe was Mama's big girl and Papa's road dog! She would happily listen to heavy metal with her dad anytime. She wasn't scared of nuthin', and she was the sweetest little girl, in her very own way. One Sunday evening there was a knock on my door, and I opened it to find my downstairs neighbor holding the tiniest little mouse in his hands. He remembered me telling him in passing how Marley pretended to be a girl to get a home, so he was now surprising me with the baby girl I never got. SURPRISE! (I can still hear Warren growling on the couch)

My neighbor had an entire apartment full of kittens that he'd rescued from a barn and he was desperately trying to find homes for them, but Warren was adamant that we weren't getting another cat. We had our two boys, and we were done. We were staying "normal."

But I couldn't just let this guy leave with her. I felt responsible for her. (Then again, I feel responsible for every animal I see.) I would keep her for the night, and I'd figure something out. I took Phoebe to her Aunt Jill's house while I did some problem solving, as my sister just lived one building over. So for the next two days my little Pheebs crashed with Aunt Jill and her cat. Then without having to do any begging, or compromising favors, out of the blue Warren said we could keep her.

So my boys had a baby sister now, and Phoebe would keep us all on our toes for the next 16 years. When she was a baby I could pick her up, hold her and carry her everywhere, but when we made the decision to be a four cat family, Phoebe stopped being so "pickable."

We added to our family one last time with baby Isabella, and Phoebe hated Isabella from the day she moved in. The feelings would become mutual, but they made it work and we were one big happy family for many, many years.

Isabella is all that is left from the original group, and she's been told she's not allowed to cross any rainbow bridges. An order has been given. That doesn't mean we're down to one cat—that's crazy talk, you rebuild!

Literally out of nowhere one evening, we found a lump on Phoebe. It wasn't there at the beginning of the day, but by bedtime, there it was. She went to the Dr. the next day, and we found out it was cancer. She was scheduled for surgery the following week, and the tumor was removed.

We thought we beat cancer, but we didn't beat cancer at all. Two months later my big girl went to sleep.

Sometimes, I wish I wouldn't have put her through the surgery at all, but you have to try right? Stupid cancer. You don't get the time you want, you make the most of the time you get, and for 16 years we got to share our lives with Phoebe. RIP big girl!

MAX POWER

We finally named a cat after a Simpsons episode. It's the one where Homer changes his name to a "name" he found on a hair dryer!

Animal rescue is a huge part of my life, and Warren's as well. I'm an across the board animal lover, but cats just seem to fit into my life better. They lay around a lot, I lay around a lot—it's a good match. The reason for primarily rescuing cats is because they are abandoned and dumped in droves. With the way they populate, it turns into an epidemic. Just in my apartment complex alone, we've rescued more kitties from the woods that circle us than I can count.

Max Power came from our very first rescue mission. Warren noticed an outside cat that was pregnant. I didn't even know he had embarked on this mission, but he was attempting to get her before she gave birth outside. We call her Big Mama, and for three months she lived in our 2nd bedroom while she gave birth and weened her babies.

Warren noticed one of her babies wasn't getting a nipple. The other two were thriving, but this little guy was barely making it. So Warren began feeding the little runt with an eyedropper, and that's how he ate every day. The plan was to get the babies big enough to leave Mama, and for everyone to get adopted. So the day came to load up the cage, and take them to the shelter.

I called Warren from work that day. I knew we really couldn't have another cat, but my heart said he was ours now. Sure enough, Warren was feeling the same way. After all, it was his TLC that kept that little baby alive. He never grew as much as his brother and sister, and he didn't have as much fur, but he was full of spunk, and his name was now Max Power.

I didn't think I'd be able to get Warren to cross the "crazy cat lady" line with me so easily!

So Mama and her two babies went to the shelter, and Max stayed behind in the house he was born in to live with his new family. We got bad news when the shelter said Mama was deemed "not" adoptable, or feral—a term I hate. We could euthanize her or we could put her back where we found her. We certainly weren't going to euthanize her, and one of the most heartbreaking scenes came that evening as we listened to her outside in the woods crying for her babies.

I'll give you the happy ending right now. As I cried along with her that night, I promised I would make it up to her and I did. We spent the next five years taking care of her and her sister, Gray Lady, outside.

We did it by building shelters and keeping them fed, until I could come up with a better plan.

When my downstairs neighbors moved away, I formulated a controversial plan, which almost made me single, but I went for it. I very recklessly went and rented their apartment, located directly under mine, and I convinced Warren that I rented it as his new office space.

He was actually looking for office space at the time, so he almost bought it, and only stayed pissed at me for less than a week. To this day Big Mama and Gray Lady are warm and comfy in their own apartment, errrrr, I mean in Warren's office.

By the way, Warren wound up loving having his office really close. He can go to work simply by walking downstairs. You're welcome!

We wouldn't have Max Power for long though, just about two years. It was a heartbreaker. We always used to joke that he didn't "cook right", and I think there was some truth to it. He had his regular Dr. visits and shots, but it just wasn't noticeable until it was too late.

One Christmas Eve I noticed that he didn't want his treats. Then on Christmas Day he was even more lethargic, so the next day he went to the vet. The news wasn't good, but it wasn't specific either. They were recommending putting him down.

But he was just a baby!?

I remember that evening having this strong feeling that we needed to go get him and bring him home. Warren made it to the shelter ten minutes before they closed. When he got home with him, little Max jumped right out of his basket. I was pleased with his energy. But cats are tricky like that. They act like everything is okay until the last minute.

Max Power died that night, in the same house he was born in, and I'm so thankful it wasn't alone in a cage. He was only given two years, but they were happy years filled with snuggles and belly smooches, and the most love you can ever get. You were a sweet little boy Max Power!

Cherish your animals, they're part of your story. They've certainly been an irreplaceable part of mine.

YE OLDE SNAPSHOT GALLERY

All Great Memories...

The Best Is Yet To Come!

ABOUT THE AUTHOR

Allyson has been a constant on Detroit's airwaves for over 2 decades. A popular television host and beloved radio host, her morning show has been a favorite not only to local listeners but to an audience across the country. Known for her strong opinions, comedic wit, and infectious laugh, Allyson entertains and inspires her fans doing what she loves most—cracking that microphone every morning to talk about it all!

She prides herself on being a strong voice for women while still maintaining her signature and organic brand of "silly."

Animal rescue is one of her greatest passions and Allyson has dedicated much of her personal and professional life to making a difference for the abandoned and abused. When not taking the media world by storm, Allyson makes time for vacuuming, reality TV, and cheese. She resides in the Ypsilanti/Ann Arbor area with her boyfriend of 23 years and various furry feline friends.

Made in the USA
Middletown, DE
18 January 2016